# The Paideia Program
## An Educational Syllabus

MORTIMER J. ADLER

# THE PAIDEIA PROGRAM

## An Educational Syllabus

Essays by the Paideia Group

Preface and introduction by
Mortimer J. Adler

Manufactured in the United States of America

1 3 5 7 9 10 8 6 4 2

Library of Congress-in-Publication Data is available.


0-02-013040-6


The Institute for Philosophical Research gratefully acknowledges
contributions from the Exxon Education Foundation, the Atlantic Richfield
Foundation, and the Joyce Foundation, to support the production and dissemination of this book
and to assist in the furtherance of the Paideia Project beyond that.

TO
JOHN AMOS COMENIUS,
who, more than 300 years ago,
envisaged the educational ideal that
*The Paideia Program* aims to realize
before the end of this century.

# Members of the Paideia Group

MORTIMER J. ADLER, *Chairman*
Director, Institute for Philosophical Research; Chairman, Board of Editors, Encyclopaedia Britannica

JACQUES BARZUN, former Provost, Columbia University; Literary Adviser, Charles Scribner's Sons, New York

OTTO BIRD, former head, General Program of Liberal Studies, University of Notre Dame, Indiana

LEON BOTSTEIN, President, Bard College, Annandale-on-Hudson, New York; President, Simon's Rock of Bard College, Great Barrington, Massachusetts

ERNEST L. BOYER, President, The Carnegie Foundation for the Advancement of Teaching, Washington, D.C.

NICHOLAS L. CAPUTI, Director, Secondary Schools, Oakland, California

DOUGLASS CATER, President, Washington College, Chestertown, Maryland; Senior Fellow, Aspen Institute for Humanistic Studies

DONALD COWAN, former President, University of Dallas; Fellow, Dallas Institute of Humanities and Culture, Texas

ALONZO A. CRIM, Superintendent, Atlanta Public Schools, Georgia

CLIFTON FADIMAN, Writer

PAUL GAGNON, Professor of Modern European History, University of Massachusetts at Boston

DENNIS GRAY, Deputy Director, Council for Basic Education, Washington, D.C.

# Contents

*Contents*

PART THREE:
THE PAIDEIA SCHOOL

# Preface

THIS BOOK completes the trilogy projected by the members of the Paideia Group to expound and explain their proposed reform of basic schooling (K through 12) in the United States.

Like its two predecessors, it is a relatively short book, designed to be read easily and quickly, and published as a paperback at a price that makes it readily accessible to the public at large.

It is intended primarily for teachers who wish to apply its precepts and recommendations in their schools and classrooms. It should be of interest also to school administrators and to those concerned with the training of teachers, to school board members, and to parents interested in the schooling of their children.

Following, as it does, *The Paideia Proposal* (1982) and *Paideia Problems and Possibilities* (1983), it does not try to persuade its readers of the soundness of the program as a whole, nor does it undertake to answer questions about its implementation in practise. The program was explained and argued for in the first Paideia book; the practical questions were answered in the second.

Like its two predecessors, *The Paideia Program* projects an ideal to be aimed at. While calling for radical departures and innovations, it allows for approximations and accommodations in implementing the ideal it sets forth.

In one important respect, this book differs from its two predecessors. It consists of a series of essays written by members of the Paideia Group, not by a single author as before. The authorship of the essays is indicated in the Table of Contents.

The individual essays have been reviewed by other members of the group and discussed by the group as a whole. These discussions did not result in complete agreement about all the recommendations made in the individual essays. Differences remained with regard to points of emphasis and matters of detail. Since the essays in this book are intended to be suggestive rather than prescriptive, we have not called attention to these minor differences, especially in view of the fact that we do not expect Paideia schools to be all alike in their adoption of the recommendations made.

For those who have not read the first two books, a brief summary of their message may be helpful. It is given in the Introduction that follows, along with a number of observations that throw light on what is distinctive about the Paideia Program. Readers will also find there some preliminary comments about the structure of this book.

We are grateful to our colleague, Jacques Barzun, for the work he did in editing the complete manuscript.

M.J.A.

# Introduction

## THE OBJECTIVES OF THE PAIDEIA PROPOSAL

THE MAIN GOAL of *The Paideia Proposal* as an educational manifesto calling for a radical reform of basic schooling in the United States is to overcome the elitism of our school system from its beginning to the present day, and to replace it with a truly democratic system that aims not only to improve the quality of basic schooling in this country, but also aims to make that quality accessible to all our children.

In 1817, Thomas Jefferson called upon the legislature of Virginia to provide all children of the state with three years of schooling at the public expense. After three years, he said, let us divide the children into those destined for labor and those destined for leisure and learning. Those destined for labor, he went on, let us send into the shops as apprentices or on to the fields as hired hands. Those destined for leisure and learning, let us send to college.

In the middle of the 19th century, Horace Mann strove to increase compulsory schooling at the public expense from three to six years. His success in this effort was not accompanied by any rejection of Jefferson's division of the children into those destined for labor and those destined for leisure and learning.

It was not until 1916, with the publication of John Dewey's *De-*

1

*mocracy and Education,* that the ideal of a democratic system of public schooling was first broached by a leading educator. In Dewey's view, all the children in our nascent democratic society have the same destiny and, therefore, should be accorded the same quality of schooling.

All the children, according to Dewey, are destined for leisure and learning as well as for labor. All have the same three elements in their futures: the demands of work, the duties of citizenship, and the obligation of each individual to make the most of himself or herself that his or her capacities allow—to lead rich and fulfilling lives. Their treatment in school should be such that it serves these three fundamental purposes for all.

The period of compulsory schooling was gradually extended during the first decades of this century from six to ten and to twelve years, but the elitism of the school system, which Dewey opposed, has not been altered to this day. We still divide the children into those destined for leisure and learning (the college bound) and those destined for labor (those not going on to college). We still have a two-track or multi-track system of schooling, where we should have a single track for all, whether or not they are going on to college when they graduate from secondary school.

*The Paideia Proposal,* published in 1982, more than sixty years after Dewey's *Democracy and Education,* made a commitment to democracy and to a democratic system of public schooling its prime objective. At that late day, the educational mandate of a democratic society was still not being discharged.

The mandate to provide equal educational opportunity for all is not discharged by giving all the same *quantity* of schooling. They must all be given the same *quality* of schooling—schooling along one and the same track, both for those not going on to college and for those going further.

Two misunderstandings of equal educational opportunity must

2

therefore be corrected. One, already mentioned, is the mistake of thinking that the same quantity of schooling suffices even though the quality is not the same for all. The other is an even more serious mistake. It consists in thinking that equality of opportunity can be expected to lead to equality of results.

The very opposite is to be expected. The equality of all the children as human beings, an equality that derives from their common humanity and personhood, is accompanied by individual inequality in talents and aptitudes.

Equality of opportunity for all conforms to the equality of all as human beings. The inequality of results that should be expected conforms to the individual inequalities that exist despite equal opportunity. Though all are given the same quality of schooling along a single track, all cannot be expected to move the same distance along that track. The ultimate outcomes will differ accordingly.

The measure or standard of accomplishment cannot, therefore, be based on the expectation of a single arithmetical equality of results. It must be based on a proportional equality of results—a mastery of what is to be learned by all to an extent that is proportionate to the individual measure of their capacity for achievement.

If the differential capacities of the children are likened to containers of different sizes, then equality of educational treatment succeeds when two results occur. First, each container should be filled to the brim, the half-pint container as well as the gallon container. Second, each container should be filled to the brim with the same quality of substance—cream of the highest attainable quality for all, not skimmed milk for some and cream for others.

When a democratic society is correctly understood to be one in which the people live under constitutional government with universal suffrage and with the securing of human rights, economic as well as political, for all citizens, it must then be recognized that

3

a democratic society is not yet fifty years old in this country. It is in its infancy. The practise of it in this country is still feeble and fragile. The establishment of a truly democratic society, in fact as well as in legislative enactments, still lies ahead of us.

Not until the second decade of this century was the female half of the population enfranchised. Not until the fifth and sixth decades were the civil rights of blacks secured. In 1910 and 1912 Theodore Roosevelt called for economic reforms to provide the working classes of this country with conditions of life that would enable them to function as good citizens. Franklin D. Roosevelt's Bill of Economic Rights was delivered to Congress in his 1944 State of the Union address.

With the advent of democratic institutions so very recent, it is not surprising that we have not yet established a democratic school system in this country. *The Paideia Proposal* calls for that achievement to be realized before the end of the century in order that our democratic institutions may be strengthened, in order that our economy may prosper, and in order that our future citizens may be able to enjoy the quality of life that should be vouchsafed every human being.

To this end, it is necessary for our people to have a correct understanding of democracy and of its commitment to equality of educational opportunity. It is also necessary to correct a number of other misunderstandings that affect our efforts to school a whole population for life in a democratic society.

FIVE ERRORS THAT NEED CORRECTION

First is the error of supposing that only some, not all, of the children are educable and that only some, not all, have a human right to aspire to become truly educated human beings in the course of their lives. We hold the very opposite: that all are ed-

4

ucable in exactly the same sense of the term, and that all have the human right to become educated in their mature years.

Second is the error of thinking that the process of education takes place and reaches completion in our educational institutions during the years of basic schooling and in advanced schooling after that. Nothing could be further from the truth. No one has ever been and no one can ever become educated in the early years of life. The reason is simply that youth itself, immaturity, is the insuperable obstacle to becoming educated. Education happens only with continued learning in adult life, after all formal schooling is over.

Third is the error of regarding teachers as the sole, primary, or principal cause of the learning that occurs in students. The truth here is that the primary, though not sole, cause of learning, whenever and wherever it occurs, is the activity of the learner's own mind. Teachers are at best only a secondary cause, an instrumental aid, assisting the process by occasioning and guiding the mental activity of the learners in their charge. This was plainly said by John Dewey at the beginning of this century when he proclaimed that all learning is by doing—any and every sort of doing that involves thinking. He did not mean just the practical operations of the sort that Dewey's followers favored in their version of what was called "the project method." Theirs was a serious misunderstanding and distortion of Dewey's maxim.

Fourth is the error of assuming that there is only one kind of learning and one kind of teaching, the kind that consists in the teacher lecturing or telling and the students learning what they hear said or find in textbook assignments. There are two other kinds—coaching and discussing—both more important than the first kind because their results are long-lasting, as the results of the first kind are not.

Fifth is the error of maintaining that schooling, basic or ad-

5

vanced, is primarily preparation for earning a living. Schooling should include that preparation, but it is the least important of the three objectives of basic schooling.

## THE DISTINCTIVE FEATURES OF THE PAIDEIA PROGRAM

The Paideia Program is concerned with all twelve years of compulsory schooling as a single integrated unit, not with the elementary grades or high school separately.

The Paideia Program, setting the same educational objectives for all, calls for the employment of the same means for achieving those objectives—a required curriculum for all, with the elimination of all particularized job-training and of all electives in the upper years. The one exception here is the requirement of a second language, with regard to which an elective choice can be made.

The Paideia Program, recognizing the pluralistic character of the public school system in this country, does not present a single specified curriculum to be uniformly adopted throughout the United States, but presents instead a curricular framework within which a variety of curriculums can be soundly constructed, appropriate to the particular circumstances of different school districts.

The Paideia Program seeks to establish a course of study that is general, not specialized; liberal, not vocational; humanistic, not technical. Only in this way can it fulfill the meaning of the words *"paideia"* and *"humanitas,"* which signify the general learning that should be in the possession of every human being.

A Paideia course of study must be so constructed that it includes all three kinds of learning and teaching, thoroughly integrated with each other.

Individual differences involving inequalities in native endowment and inequalities in nurtural or environmental backgrounds

6

call for compensatory efforts to give some children who need it pre-school preparation and, later, in the course of school years, supplementary instruction to those who need it.

A Paideia school must have a principal who is truly the principal teacher in that school, who works with the teaching staff and is their educational leader, not just the school's chief administrative officer.


THE WHAT, WHY, AND HOW OF IT

Readers of the two previous books will remember the three-column diagram that depicts the proposed framework for the desired twelve year course of study for *all* the children in our schools.

That diagram is reproduced on the following page, for examination or re-examination, because the central purpose of this book is to elucidate the elements mentioned in the diagram, to explain how learning and teaching move from one column to another.

We are here concerned with the *what,* the *why,* and the *how* of the Paideia Program: *what* is to be learned, *why* it is to be learned, and *how* it is to be learned with the help of teachers. The effort entails a radical reform—the restructuring of schools, the allocating of their funds and their facilities, the reorganization of their schedules, and their personnel.

*What* is to be learned falls under three categories: (1) kinds of knowledge to be acquired; (2) skills to be developed; and (3) understanding or insights to be achieved. We are also concerned with *why* it is to be learned, the reason in each case being the way it serves the three objectives of basic schooling—earning a living, being a good citizen, and living a full life.

*How* teachers can help their students learn what is to be learned comprises three different methods of instruction: (1) didactic teaching by lectures or through textbook assignments; (2) coach-

7

| | COLUMN ONE | COLUMN TWO | COLUMN THREE |
|---|---|---|---|
| **Goals** | ACQUISITION OF ORGANIZED KNOWLEDGE | DEVELOPMENT OF INTELLECTUAL SKILLS – SKILLS OF LEARNING | ENLARGED UNDERSTANDING OF IDEAS AND VALUES |
| | by means of | by means of | by means of |
| **Means** | DIDACTIC INSTRUCTION LECTURES AND RESPONSES TEXTBOOKS AND OTHER AIDS | COACHING, EXERCISES, AND SUPERVISED PRACTICE | MAIEUTIC OR SOCRATIC QUESTIONING AND ACTIVE PARTICIPATION |
| | in three areas of subject-matter | in the operations of | in the |
| **Areas Operations and Activities** | LANGUAGE, LITERATURE, AND THE FINE ARTS MATHEMATICS AND NATURAL SCIENCE HISTORY, GEOGRAPHY, AND SOCIAL STUDIES | READING, WRITING, SPEAKING, LISTENING CALCULATING, PROBLEM-SOLVING OBSERVING, MEASURING, ESTIMATING EXERCISING CRITICAL JUDGMENT | DISCUSSION OF BOOKS (NOT TEXTBOOKS) AND OTHER WORKS OF ART AND INVOLVEMENT IN ARTISTIC ACTIVITIES e.g., MUSIC, DRAMA, VISUAL ARTS |

THE THREE COLUMNS DO NOT CORRESPOND TO SEPARATE COURSES, NOR IS ONE KIND OF TEACHING AND LEARNING NECESSARILY CONFINED TO ANY ONE CLASS ing that forms the habits through which all skills are possessed; and (3) Socratic teaching by questioning and by conducting discussions of the answers elicited.

The second kind of learning, aided by coaching, is more important than the first, because well-formed habits of skilled performance are more desirable than the verbal memories produced by didactic instruction—the kind that enable students to pass examinations in various subject matters. The third kind of learning—understanding enlarged by Socratic questioning in seminar discussions—is even more durable.

The three chapters of Part One describe the three methods of teaching just mentioned. They also provide guidance for teachers in applying them.

For teachers to be able to use all three methods effectively, schools must be restructured, their schedules must be arranged differently from those in current practise, and their physical facilities must be put to use differently. In other words, administrative reorganization is needed to facilitate the program of teaching and learning here set forth.

In short, this book is a detailed explication of the three-column diagram. Being a static representation, the diagram cannot possibly reveal the dynamics that are indispensable to an effective execution of what it calls for—the flow back and forth of teaching and learning from one column to another.

However, words can help to do what a diagram cannot. They can describe the dynamics of the Paideia Program. Describing the dynamics, the essays in this book stress the three related and interactive aspects of the various matters with which they deal.

The importance of this cannot be overemphasized. Failure to appreciate it will lead to a serious misinterpretation of the titles of Chapters 4 through 13 in Part Two. A superficial glance at them might lead one to think that each of these chapters deals with the subject or subjects named in Column One as they are now taught in our schools—subjects about which knowledge is to be imparted by didactic teaching.

Most of these subjects are not now taught as extensively or as effectively as they should be. But the Paideia Program would not be content with a more extensive or a more effective treatment of the subjects named in those chapters. What is called for in those chapters goes much further than that. The knowledge to be acquired with the help of didactic instruction must be made secure by the skills to be developed by coaching and by the understanding to be achieved through seminar discussions on the one hand, and guided practice on the other.

Readers who reflect on what has just been said will thus not make the mistake of supposing that the titles of Chapters 4 through 13 refer to the conventional array of subjects as they are now taught didactically in our schools. Rather, those chapters suggest as strongly as can be done in short compass the modes of learning and of teaching that must be pursued to yield the educational results at which Paideia aims.

Every subject calls for more than one kind of learning and teaching, and most for all three kinds. Column Two lies at the center of the Paideia scheme—in the execution of the program, not just in its diagrammatic presentation. The range of skills to be shown there must be possessed by students to enable them to engage actively in the learning shown in Columns One and Three.

Part Three deals with the structure and organization of a Paideia school and with its distinctive features. They enable one to tell whether a particular school has adopted the Paideia Program or to assess the degree to which it is moving in that direction.

As Chapter 14 points out, the subjects in Chapters 4 through 13 must be so scheduled that all of them fit into the school day and the school year, with due differences, of course, from one grade to another in the twelve-year span. In other words, the subjects should not be allotted equal time in all twelve grades. That is manifestly impossible.

Readers should also notice that the three kinds of teaching and learning run concurrently through all twelve grades. No matter what time is given to didactic teaching, enough must be left over for coaching and for seminar discussion in every one of the twelve years, though the relative amounts will differ in the lower, middle, and upper grades.

Three subjects only will not occupy the whole twelve years: the study of a foreign language, an introduction to the world of work, and training in certain manual arts. The foreign language, for example, may be accorded four to six years; training in the manual arts, a similar time; and the introduction to the world of work may be accomplished in a single year, or two at the most.

The study of a foreign language may require instruction five times a week, but the rest need not occupy more than one or two class periods a week. This holds true also of physical training which, though required through all twelve years, need not be given every day of the week.

The Appendix contains a list of recommended readings. They are intended primarily for use in seminars, but they are no less useful in appropriate subject studies, where, however, they will tend to be regarded in the context of the subject itself—mathematics, history, literature, or whatever—rather than as works of general interest and significance, and where consideration of them will be in terms of the give-and-take proper to didactic teaching rather than a seminar discussion. They can also serve the purposes of the coaching sessions that develop linguistic, mathematical, and scientific skills.

M.J.A.

# PART ONE
# The Three Kinds of Teaching and Learning

# 1
## The Conduct of Seminars

### THE SEMINAR

PLATO'S DIALOGUES, in so many of which Socrates appears as the interlocutor, do not portray him as a seminar leader. Nor do they describe the kind of seminar discussions that should play so central a part in a Paideia school.*

In questioning those with whom he talked, Socrates sought for answers that would clarify ideas—the idea of justice, of love, of piety or virtue. He did not assign books to be read for a seminar session in which he would ask questions in order to achieve an understanding of what had been read, nor did he raise issues for the participants to argue about.

Nevertheless, it is no misrepresentation of Socrates as a special type of teacher for us to use the adjective "Socratic" as describing the method of teaching for the kind of learning shown in Column Three. Questioning students about something they have read so as to help them improve their understanding of basic ideas and

---

*Here and in the pages to follow, the phrase "a Paideia school" is used. In order to prevent misunderstanding, it must be pointed out that it is *not* used, as are such phrases as "a Magnet school" or "a Humanities school," to refer to one special type of school *among others* in a community's school system. What we have in mind when we use the phrase is a school that realizes to some appropriate degree the ideal set forth in the Paideia Program. That use of the phrase always carries with it the hope that eventually every school in the community will be, or be on its way to becoming, a Paideia school.   M.J.A.

values is a procedure that can appropriately be called Socratic.

In Plato's dialogues, Socrates never teaches didactically, for he persistently claims that he does not know enough to do that. Nor does he coach anyone, except indirectly, to help them become more skillful in the use of their minds. He describes himself as an inquiring teacher, one who asks questions and pursues answers to get at the truth. He called his method of teaching something like midwifery because he viewed it as assisting the labor of his companions in giving birth to ideas.

The materials for seminar discussions may be either books or other products of human art. If books, they must be books that present ideas or broach issues, not books that are catalogues of information or direct expositions of factual knowledge. Discussable books are the very opposite of text-books; these last are essentially undiscussable, because they are designed as instruments of didactic instruction.*

Here, as in other chapters, it is important to keep in mind the difference between the lower and upper levels of basic schooling—the pre-departmental and the departmentalized grades.

At the lower level, where the classroom teacher engages in all three kinds of teaching, seminar-like discussions should occur much more frequently than at the upper level, perhaps every day, though only for relatively brief spans—at most a half hour or so for the very young, and a little more for those who are older.

Such seminar-like discussions at this level need not require much, if any, assigned reading in advance. They may be based on other subjects being taught in a given class. They may be about a story told by the teacher or some other material presented orally by the teacher, as in kindergarten or the first grade. From the third or fourth grade on, they can be based on short and simple reading

---

*For recommended readings usable in seminar discussions, consult the Appendix (see pp. 185–238).

assignments. In any case, they will differ from other work by being conversations in which teachers and students engage in an informal manner, exchanging opinions and even arguing with one another about what has been said or read.

At the upper level, seminars should occur less frequently, once a week or at most twice a week, depending on the character and length of the book to be read in advance. They should never run less than ninety minutes and should usually run for two hours.

At the lower level, the children ordinarily do not move from one classroom to another in the course of a day. But the classroom in which they are coached in skills or in which they receive didactic instruction is not suitable for seminar discussions. These should occur with all the participants—both teachers and students—sitting so that they can face one another as they talk to one another.

Seminar discussions, even at the lower level of basic schooling, cannot be carried on in a room in which children sit in rows from front to back and the teacher stands or sits in front of the first row. Fortunately, many modern classrooms are equipped with movable chairs which permit the teacher to arrange the kind of configuration needed for carrying on a conversation. Elsewhere, a special room so equipped will be needed.

For students in the upper grades, special rooms must similarly be furnished with a hollow-square table and movable chairs for seminar discussions. Just as they move from one classroom to another for didactic instruction in different subjects, so they will move to the seminar room for Socratic teaching.

Let us consider what seminars are and what they are not. What they are can be described in a single word: they are *conversations*, conducted in an orderly manner by the teacher who acts as leader or moderator of the discussion.

Conversations differ from quizzes in which teachers ask students questions in order to test reading done and to put scores against their names in the grade books. Conversations are not concealed lectures in which teachers ask questions for rhetorical purposes only, answering the questions themselves rather than patiently soliciting answers from students. Conversations are not the kind of question-and-answer sessions described in Chapter 3, which should always follow a period of didactic instruction to make sure that students are actively using their minds to understand the unit of organized knowledge that the didactic teacher is presenting at that time.

The role of the Socratic teacher in a seminar is that of a good conversationalist who primes the pump of discussion by asking leading questions and pursuing the answers given to them by asking more questions. The Socratic teacher thus leads the discussion, but he also acts as moderator in the sense that he or she must exercise control over it; he has the duty to keep it on the track and keep it moving along that track.

It is often difficult to both lead and moderate, to ask leading questions and to watch closely in what direction the conversation is going. For that reason the ideal seminar should have two leaders, or moderators, one of whom will talk while the other listens and vice versa. One leader may play the more outspoken role for one hour, perhaps, then the other takes over, or both exchange parts more frequently, though they should never fall into a dialogue before a silent audience. An experienced Socratic teacher can conduct a good seminar alone, and that is likely to be the most common situation in a Paideia school.

## DIFFERENT KINDS OF SEMINARS FOR DIFFERENT KINDS OF BOOKS

The primary goal of Socratic teaching, whether in a formal seminar or not, is to bring out and then clarify the ideas and is-

18

sues that are raised by something that has been read or otherwise experienced jointly by the leader and the students. A secondary goal of such teaching is to make clear the book or work of art itself.

A seminar leader who wants only to reveal his superior knowledge by telling the students what is in a particular book or play or other work is not a Socratic teacher. He is only a disguised didactic teacher and whoever does this does not need the time and the paraphernalia of a seminar. He might as well stand up in front of the class and lecture.

The ideas and issues raised by good books are more permanent and more interesting than those that are raised by inferior books. In fact, the best books—great books, as they are called—raise the most fundamental and lively issues of all.

The best seminars occur when a leader or leaders join with students in examining the issues and questions raised by great books. In the upshot the issues should become clear; but it should also become clear that each participant, leader or student, has a responsibility to face those issues as they affect himself or herself.

In such a seminar the leader is not a teacher in the ordinary sense. He or she is merely the first among equals in a joint effort to reach a goal that is shared by all.

Books differ, and so do seminars that deal with them. Imaginative literature—fiction, drama, poetry—constitutes one main type of book. Expository literature—science, history, philosophy—constitutes the other main type.

A seminar about Shakespeare's *Hamlet,* for example, is different from a seminar about Aristotle's *Ethics.* An able seminar leader conducts the two seminars in different ways.

With both books, the first task is to understand what has been read. In the *Ethics,* the first step is to examine the statements that Aristotle makes, the conclusions that he draws, and the advice he gives, more or less explicitly, about how to live our lives. In *Hamlet* the first step is to make sure that all the participants understand what happens in the play and why it happens when it does.

In the *Ethics,* only after the points that Aristotle makes are well understood is it appropriate to begin discussing whether his conclusions are true, or whether his advice is good. Similarly, in *Hamlet,* only when the language and plot of the play are well understood is it appropriate to consider what relevance the story has, if any, to our own lives.

The goal is the same in both cases: to bring out the basic ideas or issues that Aristotle, on the one hand, and Shakespeare, on the other hand, force us to face if we read their books well. But the conduct of the discussion—the kind of questions asked—is bound to differ.

In the *Ethics,* or any other expository book, the questions asked by the leader tend to be linear, forming a sequence with an established aim in view. *Hamlet,* however, like other works of imaginative literature, cannot be approached in that fashion without missing much that is essential.

The "secret" of *Hamlet* really is a secret, and there is no one line of questioning that will arrive at it. Rather, the seminar leader must circle round and round the play, seeking for an opening here, for an opportunity there, for a point that it would be helpful to make at this stage of the conversation.

For this reason, seminar discussions of imaginative works often seem more chaotic, less orderly, than discussions of expository works. At the same time, the discussions of imaginative works are often more moving and affecting for all concerned.

The important questions that arise in a seminar, it cannot be repeated too often, are the questions to which there is no "right" answer. Many other kinds of questions must be asked, of course. In the *Ethics,* to take that example again, there are questions of fact that a good leader will ask. What, in Aristotle's view, is the definition of virtue? Why is courage a virtue, foolhardiness not? What are the characteristics of a happy life? Is happiness the same as pleasure or contentment? If not, why not? These are questions to which there are right and wrong answers, because Aristotle says one definite thing on each of these subjects.

Similarly for *Hamlet,* there are questions to which there are right answers, and it will be useful to ask them. Why does Polonius warn his daughter Ophelia against Prince Hamlet? When Hamlet comes upon Ophelia in the gallery, has he overheard Polonius and King Claudius plotting to enable the younger pair to meet and talk? When they meet, does he know they are being overheard? And so with scores of other factual matters.

Those questions are very different from such others as the following. Does Hamlet love Ophelia, or only desire her? Does he believe what the Ghost of his father tells him? Why does he pretend to be mad? Is it, as Polonius suggests, because he is in love? Why is Hamlet so concerned about his mother's marriage to the king?

These are questions to which there are no definitive answers, and for that very reason they are important questions.

Turn back once more to the *Ethics*. Are there any rules of conduct that, if followed, will lead to moral virtue—in other words, how does one become virtuous? How does one teach someone else—for example, how should a father teach his son—to be so? Can virtue be taught at all? Is it ever appropriate to say, "I am happy"? And what of your own answer to that question? Is it the same as Aristotle's? Who is right? Such questions should be asked toward the end of the seminar, at the point where it is fairly clear that all the participants understand the book, but are puzzling about its meaning and relevance to human life.

In a Paideia school, Socratic teaching starts in kindergarten and continues throughout all twelve years of basic schooling. The main change, aside from the increasing maturity of the conversation, is in the frequency of seminars and the amount of time devoted to each. Even so, the questions, ideas, and issues themselves do not greatly change as the years pass. It is wrong to think that young children are only capable of considering and talking about "simple" ideas and issues. Justice, for example, is not a simple idea, and yet it is one that very young children are even more interested in than older ones. What is fair? Why is fairness important and desirable? Is it fair to punish someone who has done wrong?

Such profound questions may arise at any moment in the lives of young children and can properly come up in the course of a discussion with them. The good teacher will take advantage of such moments to lead the conversation a little farther than it would naturally go without being too demanding. But if he or she fosters a concern with such matters in young children, those same youngsters will turn out excellent participants in seminars in the upper grades.

Not all seminars are, strictly speaking, discussions, just as not all materials are books. Although it is generally true that the inability to state one's ideas or beliefs is a sign that one's ideas or beliefs are vague and ill-understood, this is not so of all ideas and beliefs. What ideas are being considered or treated in Mozart's G minor symphony? Would it ever be appropriate to say *in words* what those ideas are? Is there not some other form of response to Mozart that is more appropriate than speaking?

Looking at a painting by Cézanne, one can describe what one sees, but is this the most appropriate response? Which is more important, the painting itself or the feelings evoked by it in a viewer? Or is the relation and tension between those two things what is important? And is this fruitfully discussable? If the goal

22

in discussing *Hamlet* is to understand both the play and its meaning for us, would it be more fruitful to put a production of the play on the stage than to talk about it? And does not something happen, when a group of people dance together, that is totally beyond any statement in words?

In a Paideia school many kinds of seminars will take place during the twelve years of basic schooling. Teachers will lead them in different ways, and striking innovations will be made from time to time. But all seminars will have one thing in common. They will always be joint searches. The very best seminars, the ones that both leaders and students will remember for years, perhaps for a lifetime, will be those in which something new and unexpected was discovered. This is true for the leaders as well as the students. It would be a very unsuccessful seminar leader who was never surprised.

HOW TO BE AN EFFECTIVE SEMINAR LEADER

The task of the seminar leader or moderator is threefold: to ask a series of questions that define the discussion and give it direction; to examine or query the answers by trying to draw out the reasons for them or the implications they have; and to engage the participants in two-way talk with one another when the views they have advanced appear to be in conflict.

In order to perform the second and third of these tasks, the seminar leader must be as exact in listening as in questioning. This is the moderator's most important obligation and one that is difficult to discharge. The moderator must often rephrase something said by a student in order to make it clear to everyone else around the table. To do that well requires listening with the mind, not just with the ear. Great energy must be expended in asking good questions and in listening with penetration. That is why no teacher should ever be required to conduct more than one seminar a day.

To ask questions productively means to reformulate the same question in a variety of ways, trying one phrasing after another until the question truly catches the mind not only of the student interrogated, but of all the others. The teacher is not performing as a leader or moderator if he just sits back and acts as chairman of the meeting, inviting the participants to say whatever is on their minds, one after another. The result then is not a seminar but a rap session.

The kind of learning that should occur in a seminar stems from the kind of questions asked. They should be questions that raise issues, questions that lead to further questions when answers are given, and seldom questions that can be answered by a simple yes or no. Such simple questions may of course have to be interlaced with others in the course of the seminar, to serve as transitions or bridges between larger questions and answers.

Hypothetical questions are often useful, helping to uncover the consequences of one or another supposition being considered. When complex questions are asked, attention should also be called to their subordinate parts, each to be taken into account or separately discussed in sequence.

Most important of all, the seminar leader must make sure that the questions asked are heard and understood. Questions are never to be taken as signals for the interrogated to respond by saying whatever is on their minds at the moment. When that occurs, seminar leaders must repeat the question and insist on its being answered with relevance, and persist until answers to the point are given. Students should be told that they are never to answer a question they do not understand. They, too, should persist in demanding that the seminar leader rephrase the question until they grasp its meaning.

Seminar leaders should not accept half-minded listening on the part of students or put up with garbled, incoherent speech in their replies. Neither should they rest content with statements that appear to be generally acceptable without also seeking for the reasons that underlie them or the consequences that follow from them. When students give answers that are unsatisfactory in any way, the seminar leader has an easier task than when students give answers that are, on the surface, satisfactory. It is easier to ask further questions that uncover what is unsatisfactory about an answer given; much harder to ask further questions to dig below the surface of an apparently satisfactory answer and discover whether the student who gave it was merely mouthing words or really expressing thoughts.

The state of mind that teachers and students alike bring to a seminar is an important element in its being effective teaching and learning. Those engaged in a discussion must always be prepared to change their minds as a result of what occurs in the course of it. They should be open to views that are new to them. They should be willing to consider such new opinions, and not be stubbornly resistant to something they have never thought of before, but they should not be passively submissive and accept all they hear, either.

Seminar leaders must take measures to control students who are stubbornly contentious or disputatious, who argue for the sake of arguing, and are more interested in winning an argument than in discovering the merits of opposite views. Contrariwise, they should challenge students who are indifferent, toplofty in their silent detachment, acquiescent and uncritical.

In didactic teaching and also in coaching, teachers have knowl-

25

edge or skills not possessed by their students. This contributes to their competence as teachers. The competence of seminar leaders cannot be measured in the same way. The teacher as seminar leader should simply be a more alert inquirer and learner than the students—more astute in the effort to understand whatever materials are being discussed, more adroit in doing this by means of intelligent conversation.

It would be a great mistake for seminar leaders to regard themselves as competent by virtue of knowing the right answers to the questions they ask and explore. As we have observed, the very best questions for seminar purposes are ones to which there is no single correct answer, but rather many answers that compete for attention, understanding, and judgment. The discussion leader's competence therefore consists in awareness of what questions are important, what range of answers deserve consideration and demand judgment.

Here are a few further recommendations and suggestions for those who wish to perform effectively as seminar leaders. The suggestions apply especially to seminars in which expository books are discussed. Some concern what teachers should do to prepare themselves; others touch on matters not yet mentioned that can make seminars more effective or less.

First, and most important, the leader prepares for a seminar on an expository work by reading that work as carefully as possible, pencil in hand. He or she underlines all the crucial words whose precise meaning must be kept in mind and marks the pivotal sentences or paragraphs in which the author states his underlying theses succinctly, argues for them, or raises questions about them. The thorough reader also makes marginal notes of all sorts about the connections between one part of the text and another.

Next, the leader draws up a list of the important points, questions, and issues that occur to him as materials for discussion.

26

Then, after going over the list, he or she puts down a very small number of questions, phrased with great care, which are to be the backbone of the two-hour discussion. Sometimes just one question will suffice for the whole two hours; sometimes three or four are needed; seldom, if ever, more than five.

If more than one, the questions should be ordered so that the first opens up matters to be further explored by the second; the second leads to further explorations by the third question; and so on. In addition, the questions should be such as anyone in the group might be expected to answer; the best opening question is one that everyone around the table can be asked to answer in succession. The leader should seldom be satisfied with the answers given. The leader must always ask, Why? Or: Is that all you think is involved? Who can add an essential point? Is not the second part overstated? Is ____ the right word for ____? And so on. All this implies that a student's answer should be required to hit the bull's eye sooner or later; that the student's statement be grammatically correct and that it be uttered in clear and complete sentences.

Above all, the leader should not allow a key word to be used ambiguously or loosely. No one can legislate about how words should be used; but if two students use a given word in different senses, or if a student uses a word used by the author or by the moderator in a different sense, that difference in sense should be plainly recognized and labeled before the discussion proceeds. Efforts should be made to have the participants come to terms with one another by agreeing, for the time being at least, on how key words will be used.

As the discussion gets going, conflicting answers to a given question will begin to emerge, and the moderator must then make everyone explicitly aware of the issue that is being joined. Unless the conflict is clearly formulated and fully understood, it is futile to carry on the debate. To aid such formulation and debate, the leader may use the blackboard, putting on it some form of diagram that frames the issue and indicates the opposing positions on it, thus enabling the students to identify the position they are taking or the view they are defending.

After conducting several seminars on the same book, the leader may often be able to anticipate key issues, construct appropriate diagrams, and put them on the blackboard before the discussion begins. When thus presented in schematic form, the diagrams may employ symbols that will at first appear to be mere hieroglyphics to the student but will become intelligible after the discussion has reached a certain point.

Great human issues and proposed answers are not confined each to one great book. So in a series of seminars with the same group of students, whatever understanding has been achieved in an earlier session should be used in dealing with questions or issues raised in later sessions. It follows that a good ordering of the reading materials is as important as their proper selection in the first place.

The leader must never talk down to the students or treat them as most teachers do when addressing them in a class session. The leader must make an even greater effort to understand what is going on in the mind of another human being who, younger and less experienced, is struggling to understand something that is difficult for anyone of any age to understand.

The leader should be patient and polite in dealing with everyone around the table—as patient and polite as one is with guests at one's dinner table. The leader should set an example of intellectual etiquette that the participants may learn from and imitate. Above all, the leader should conduct the whole discussion with a smile and produce laughter whenever it feels spontaneous and relevant. Nothing is more conducive to learning than wit and laughter, though naturally the laughter is *never* at a student's expense.

## HOW TO BECOME AN EFFECTIVE SEMINAR LEADER

All of the foregoing recommendations or suggestions to teachers who wish to *be* effective seminar leaders do not, by themselves, suffice as means for *becoming* so. The Socratic conduct of discussions calls for skills that, like every other skill, can be acquired only through performance under supervision.

Knowing a set of pedagogical rules never produces teachers who can perform effectively in any of the three modes of teaching, any more than knowing the rules for driving automobiles or cooking food produces good drivers or good cooks. Good habits of doing must be acquired. They can be acquired only by practice under the supervision of a good performer.

This amounts to saying that teachers will become effective seminar leaders only in the course of time, through the efforts they make in conducting seminars with an experienced leader present, who will later point out their mistakes and how to correct them. For example, he will say that they asked too many questions one after another instead of pursuing the answer to one question by questioning the student's first answer.

Beginning seminar leaders should be present as observers of seminars conducted by teachers who already possess the habits of good performance. Observing on one occasion will seldom be enough. A number of seminars, differing in the character of the books read should be observed, and the observers should have a chance to ask the leader why this or that was done. The other prerequisite for beginners is to participate in seminars as stu-

29

dents. In no other way can they fully appreciate what is involved in learning from questions and answers and thus discover how best to question.

Available technology makes the first of these prerequisites generally available. The conduct of seminars by effective discussion leaders can be televised and made widely accessible through video cassettes. The distribution of these might be accompanied by printed materials, including transcripts of the discussion, copies of the reading materials discussed, and comments by an effective leader on the seminar to be observed by the novice.

## SEMINARS IN RELATION TO COACHING
## AND DIDACTIC INSTRUCTION

Seminars can be used to reinforce coaching in a variety of ways. When well-conducted, seminars involve coaching in the arts of reading, of speaking, and of listening. Students in such seminars have their attention drawn to deficiencies in those three functions of the mind and are told how to improve or correct them. In addition, seminars may be accompanied by a writing assignment. Students who have read something in preparation for a seminar should certainly have their understanding of what they read altered by the discussion. Hence they can be asked to write a brief essay recording to what extent and by what means their understanding was changed.

These essays can then be criticized by a writing coach. They may have to be rewritten. They can also be made the subject of interrogation, in which a speaking coach requires the students to explain and defend this or that point in the essay. This coaching requires them to speak well and listen well. When this is done time after time, the coaching aspect of the seminar should improve a student's skills in all four of the language arts—reading, writing, speaking, and listening.

On matters taught didactically, the books read and discussed in seminars may incite students to ask their didactic teachers questions. That might never have occurred to them otherwise. This improves the learning that didactic teaching is concerned with, making the learner's mind more active. It helps to prevent the merely verbal memorization of teacher talk that students tend to be satisfied with in class.

This chapter has concentrated on the discussion of books. Seminars about other materials are treated in other chapters, and other chapters will also comment on how the teaching of the subjects with which they are concerned—scientific, mathematical, historical—can be advanced by discussion.

M.J.A. & C.V.D.

# 2
# Coaching

## COACHING IN A PAIDEIA CLASSROOM

### FIRST EXAMPLE*

A ninth grade algebra class. Carl writes on the chalk board:

$$2x + 6 = 8$$
$$2x = 2$$
$$x = 0$$

Carl's teacher: *Carl, check it for me.*

$$2(0) + 6 = 8$$
$$0 + 6 = 8$$
$$6 = 8$$

Carl: (pause) It doesn't work.

*Write out your steps.*

$$2x + 6 = 8$$
$$(2x + 6) - 6 = (8) - 6$$

---

*This and the second example illustrate the kind of coaching that occurs in what might be called a tutorial session: one student being persistently questioned and led on from point to point while other students observe the process. Such tutorial sessions differ strikingly from seminars in which all students engage together in discussion.

There are forms of coaching in which students are made to practise under supervision until their performance is satisfactory. This aims to produce the habit of the requisite skill. Yet other forms of coaching involve group discussion, as exemplified in the third example. One can see there how coaching, questioning, and telling inevitably interweave as a class of this sort proceeds.   M.J.A.

$$\frac{2x}{2} = \frac{2}{2}$$

$$x = 0$$

*When you divide 2 by itself, do you get zero?*

Umm.

*Write it out.*

$$2 \overline{)\ 2} \atop \phantom{2)}\underline{\ 2}$$

*So . . .*

One.

*Right! Now go back to your problem.*

$$2x + 6 = 8$$
$$(2x + 6) - 6 = (8) - 6$$
$$2x = 2$$
$$x = 1$$

*So far so good. Now give it another check.*

$$2(1) + 6 = 8$$
$$2 + 6 = 8$$
$$8 = 8$$

It works.

*Why does it work?*

I subtracted 6 from each side of the equation.

*Yes . . . and you divided 2 by itself properly . . . Now, could you solve this equation another way?*

Umm.

*Try.*

(A long pause. Doodling on the chalk board.)

*Remember, as long as one treats each side of the equation similarly, one can perform unlimited operations . . . you tried subtraction, and it helped you to solve the problem. Could some other operation work equally well?*

(A pause. Scribbling.) Take 2 out.

*What's that mean?*

You know, take it out.

*You mean, subtract 2 from each side?*

No, divide by 2.

*Write it out . . . now, let's see your work.*

$$2x + 6 = 8$$
$$2(x + 3) = 2(4)$$
$$\frac{2(x + 3)}{2} = \frac{2(4)}{2}$$
$$x + 3 = 4$$
$$x = 1$$

*So . . . it works. But it didn't work for Eddie here. Look at Eddie's problem and tell him why.*

(Eddie's solution, adjacent on the chalkboard.)

$$2x + 6 = 8$$
$$\frac{2x + 6}{2} = \frac{\overset{4}{8}}{2}$$
$$x + 6 = 4$$
$$x = 4 - 6$$
$$x = -2$$

34

Umm . . . it *should* work.

*But it doesn't, and yours did. Why?*

You see . . . the 6. It should be three.

*Ok . . . now, here's another one: 10 + 2x = 30 . . . Eddie, show Carl how to do it.*

Carl (with Eddie) is being coached. He's learning algebra—a mathematical skill—but he is also learning about observing, calculating and about how to trouble-shoot, how to identify errors and figure out what caused them. He is learning, fundamentally, how to think—logically, resourcefully, and imaginatively.

One learns such skills only by experience, in essence by trial and error. Teachers can greatly improve the efficiency and accuracy of that process by *coaching,* by a judicious mixture of telling (". . . as long as one treats each side of the equation similarly, one can perform unlimited operations . . .") and simple "questioning" ("Why must he divide the 6 by the 2?").

By an artful blend of information, challenge, drill ("here's another one . . .") and encouragement ("Right! . . ."), the teacher helps the student see the order in (say) algebra and to habituate himself in the right steps and motions so as to perform these simple intellectual operations.

Throughout, the student is the key worker and the subject matter is the stuff with which he is developing his skills. The emphasis in a coaching situation is on the student getting his ideas to work accurately and then practicing the skill. Most often, this is a slow, tedious, patience-testing process.

### SECOND EXAMPLE

The assignment:  *a paragraph about your grandparents.*

Angela (a young and insecure eleven-year-old) writes:

My grandmother is Polish. My grandfather Latvian. They <u>dont</u> know English until 21, though I am an American. <u>Dads</u> Dad is German. Mom's is <u>Latvin</u>. <u>There</u> foreigners. They went to school together.

*Angela, that's interesting! All your grandparents came from across the Atlantic! And some of them went to school together. Is that how they met?*

I don't know.

*I want you to look at your paragraph again with me. I want you to check the spelling of the words I've underlined and I want you to check again to see that each sentence in the paragraph has a noun and a verb.*

Umm.

*The reader understands better when there are complete sentences. One of yours isn't complete. Which one?*

(Pause) The second one.

*Why?*

There's no "is".

*Right. And that third sentence doesn't sound correct either?*

No . . . but I can fix it.

*Good. Can the reader tell just where each grandparent came from?*

Yes . . . ummm . . . No.

*Ok. Who went to school together?*

Grandmoms.

36

*You'll want to make that clear. And think of what the best or-*
*der of the sentence might be to tell the reader your story and to*
*highlight what you think is important.*

Umm.

*Now, write it again.*

(In due course)

I am an American. My grandparents are foreigners. My
mother's Mom came from *Poleand*. My mother's Dad came
from Latvia. My father's Mom came from Poland. My father's
Dad came from Germany. They didn't speak until they were
21. My *grandmother's* went to school together. No grandparent *new* English until they grew up.

*This is better. You are telling me, the reader, that you are an*
*American but your grandparents are, or were, foreigners. Inter-*
*esting. Do you think others in this class also had four foreign-*
*born grandparents?* (A brief digression. Angela becomes sort of a
heroine, with all four grandparents from the old countries. Then,
back privately to Angela.) *What about the underlined words?*

(She reads silently) But "grandmother's" is right!

*Really?* (a skeptical tone)

Yes . . . (pause) uh-oh. The apostrophe, or whatever you call
it?

*Exactly. Now look at this last sentence. Is there a trap there?*

(Pause)

*What little word hides behind "no . . ."?*

(Puzzlement)

*No "one" grandparent.*

Umm. What's wrong?

*Read the sentence, with the hidden word out for us to hear.*

"No one grandparent knew English until they grew up."

*So . . .*

(Long pause) . . . Oh, "they."

*Exactly! Now, how should it read?*

"No grandparent knew English until he grew up."

*Good . . . and they did "speak" something before age 21, didn't they! (smile) . . . OK . . . Are your grandparents all "he's"?*

No . . . so you mean I have to say "until she or he grew up"?

*You don't have to; "he" can stand for both males and females. But people today often like to use "he and she." It suggests we don't seem to forget the grandmoms! Now, read the paragraph to me.*

(Angela reads)

*Clump. Clump. Clump. Why does it thump so much?*

Umm . . . it does go that way . . . what should I do?

*"Variety is the spice of life."*

What?

*Think! Write me a new paragraph.*

(In due course)

38

Although I am an American, all four of my grandparents were born and raised in foreign countries. Both of my grandmothers came from Poland. Surprising to say, they even went to the same school together! My mother's father, though, was Latvian, and my Dad's father was German. No one of my grandparents spoke English until she or he was over twenty-one years old.

Again, here we had telling and simple questioning. The "coaching" was central, though. Throughout the substance of study was Angela's own work, her own expression, her own thinking. The point of this exercise was to help her express herself clearly; to become a habitual, probing questioner of her own expression; to put herself in the reader's position.

She was expected to get her spelling right, though (in this instance) she was shown where her spelling errors might be. She was criticized sharply, if gingerly, but also praised, legitimately.

Not all of her mistakes were identified at once. Her teacher carefully selected what to challenge, knowing that all errors do not disappear in one fell swoop. She was asked repeatedly to do her work over. In a word, she was drilled in the formation of good habits, of revision, honestly but with enough endorsing praise that she did not lose heart.

SOME MAXIMS FOR THE GUIDANCE OF COACHING

To quote *The Paideia Proposal:* ". . . an important end of schools is the development of intellectual skills—skills of learning by means of reading, writing, speaking, listening, calculating, problem-solving, observing, measuring, estimating . . . exercising critical judgment. These skills are the ones everyone needs in order to learn anything, in school or elsewhere." Skill training is "the

39

backbone of basic schooling." In order to coach effectively, several conditions are essential.

*First*, the teacher must know the student, and how he or she thinks, attacks a problem, confuses things, loses or does not lose heart. While there are general patterns in the learning of skills, the exceptions to these patterns are frequent. Effective coaching takes effect one-to-one. In essence, it is a kind of individual tutoring, a lively conversation about one's skills. Still, much time must also be spent by the student, alone, struggling things through.

Good teachers so arrange their classes that this one-to-one discussion can take place while the other students work quietly on their own. Or the one-to-one can become one-to-three, or five, assuming that the three or five show roughly the same successes or errors on their papers or analogous work.

The one-to-one encounter is particularly well occasioned by written work: each student "converses" with his or her teacher by means of a paper turned in, analyzed and criticized in writing by the teacher and then returned. Sometimes the teacher can usefully coach himself in public, to provide a model. The music teacher can play the tune on his recorder and ask the students to criticize him, the supposed expert. He then critiques himself, thus showing both the points to which students should be attentive and that criticism is also applicable to teachers.

Sometimes another student can be an excellent coach, assuming that student's competence. Some of us prefer to expose our errors to our peers rather than to our elders. A well-designed computer program can also be a "coach"; the impersonality of this interactive machine can be an asset, at least some of the time.

Sometimes entire groups of students can be coached simultaneously. The teacher, for example, can present one student's sentence to a whole class by means of an overhead projector and critique it for all to see. An entire group can speak together in pattern

40

drills in language class. However, the usefulness of this process is limited. We do not learn to improve *our* serve in tennis very well by observing another's being criticized. Individual attention by the coach is crucial.

*Second,* the material of coaching is the student's work, in which skill is displayed for the teacher to criticize. A non-communicative child, or a child who is never asked to explain himself or otherwise exhibit his skill, or a child so fearful of exposing his inadequacies that he tries to hide them, cannot be coached. One cannot help a quarterback become a better passer if one can never see him try to throw the ball.

It takes time—and often courage—for each student to exhibit his or her skills. No two students will progress at precisely the same rate. They catch on in different ways and at different times. This makes a class awkward for the good teacher.

And it may take time to bring some students to the point that they will *want* to be coached, will desire to struggle with their work as Carl and Angela did. Intellectual pressure—which is what much coaching is—is threatening and felt by many contemporary American youngsters (alas) to be foreign and thus deemed irrelevant. These young citizens are all too often comfortable with unexamined images, ideas in the form of mere headlines. (This is truer of older rather than younger students, a sad testimony of the impact of our culture.) As a result, many teachers will have to inveigle, cajole and inspire young people into a frame of mind which will permit coaching. Wise instructors never underestimate the challenge of this preparatory task. Without its completion, frustrated failure is almost assured. As with coaching itself, it proceeds one-by-one, but the attitude of peers is crucial. (If some of the most influential students engage, most of the others will follow.)

*Third,* immediacy is crucial. If Carl had turned in his $x = 0$ paper and did not get it back for a week, the benefit of dialogue would be lost. Again, this imperative has consequences for the organization of the school day. Teachers *must* have time to correct student work thoroughly and promptly.

*Fourth,* shrewd criticism by the teacher is essential. Simply telling Carl that his first answer was wrong does not help him learn much. *Why* it was wrong is what teaches. The teacher has to spot the error. Its identification and description in a form and sequence that the student understands is a demanding task.

*Fifth,* different subjects at different levels require more or less coaching, and varying techniques. Flash card exercises with seven-year-olds and laboratory exercises for seventeen-year-olds (the coaching being a critique of how each student tackles the problem to be solved) are quite different things. However, while the intensity and frequency of coaching might vary over time, the approach is the same with younger or older minds and with subject matter of any sort. Only the level of abstraction varies. The focus is on how the student employs his mind, whether that student is in kindergarten or the twelfth grade.

*Sixth,* often painful, usually boring, drill is necessary ("write it again . . ."). Students have to develop error-free habits. Repeating the act—i.e. experience—is indispensable. The teacher must be patient and realize that unless the student does the work, little or no useful effect follows. Merely telling Angela how to order her sentences gives her no practice in sentence arranging. Of course, the final product may look better if the teacher tells Angela just what to do. (One must, therefore, always be skeptical of displays of students' work on the walls of teacher-dominated classrooms.)

*Seventh,* coaching requires time and a class small enough so that a teacher can learn how each pupil's mind works. This is more likely to happen in good elementary schools today, thanks to their simple structure. It is less likely to occur in most Ameri-

42

can secondary schools, where teachers are often faced with well over a hundred students. These appear in class for relatively brief periods of time and are served up a curriculum that emphasizes coverage of information: world history from the Pharaohs to the Falklands, in 180 class periods. How could this lead to the rigorous, resourceful use of the mind?

Good coaching simply cannot be done in the intellectually fragmented over-busy typical high school. The time for patient, often dogged dialogue is not there. There is little incentive for time-absorbing drill ("write that paper once more"). The opportunities for coaching are few—save on the athletic field, in good special education programs, or (for more advantaged youngsters) at the consoles of their home computers.

### THIRD EXAMPLE

A twelfth grade student, Sam, starts:

How come we dropped that bomb on Hiroshima? Awful! (The assignment had been to read John Hersey's *Hiroshima*.)

Another student: They deserved it.

And another: More people were killed earlier in a raid on Tokyo . . .

*What's the evidence on that Tokyo bomber raid?* The teacher queries.

Hiroshima was worse.

*What do you mean by 'worse'?*

More people were killed.

*At one moment, from one raid?*

43

Yes.

*What's the evidence?*

Umm.

*Where can you find out?*

The World Almanac?

*Perhaps. Where would the Almanac get its data, though?*

Air Force records?

*Yes. And the "official" histories of World War II by American and Japanese authorities . . . The governments sponsored detailed studies of the battles . . . Bill, get the Almanac . . . what does it say?*

(In due course) The Tokyo fire-bombing raid killed more people.

(Mary) But Hiroshima was worse!

*Why?*

It was an atomic bomb!

(The class wag) You're dead either way, Mary dear!

(laughter, abruptly ending)

*Who decided to use the atomic bomb . . . Agnes?*

MacArthur.

*Is she correct, Carlos?*

No . . . it was Harry Truman.

*How do you know?*

44

He was the Commander-in-Chief.

*Fine . . . but does that mean he made this particular decision?*

(Silence)

*Carlos?*

Well . . . he did.

*How might you prove it?*

Get copies of Truman's orders? His diaries?

*Yes. Truman wrote his memoirs. He records the route he took to reach a decision . . . But can you always trust a person's diary?*

(Laughter)

*You'd have to check Truman's recollections with those of others, and with official documents, orders to the Air Force . . .*

It was a cruel thing to do. That book told it. (Mary talking, again, of Hersey's *Hiroshima*.)

*How do you mean "cruel," Mary?*

Lots of people died.

*Truman believed that if we dropped this bomb, killing many people, the Japanese would be so frightened that they would surrender now, thus saving ultimately many more lives.*

(Silence)

*Was he right?*

Yes. . . . Well, no.

45

*The Three Kinds of Teaching and Learning*

*How can one find out?*

One can't. It's all just a guess.

*How did Truman make his guess?*

. . . (The discussion continues. In due course:)

The class is almost over. *For homework, write for me a one-page essay defining "cruelty," and assess to what extent President Truman was or was not "cruel," by your definition, in ordering the dropping of the Hiroshima bomb.*

Coaching is here: the habits of using evidence ("what's the evidence on that Tokyo raid?"); precision in the use of words ("what do you mean by 'worse'?"); sequential logic (". . . does that mean he made this particular decision?").

Didactic instruction and Socratic questioning are here also. The three kinds of teaching can never be wholly segregated. Students were gaining new information: the existence of a fire-bomb raid on Tokyo before Hiroshima. They were developing understanding: the myriad meanings of the concept of cruelty.

Central to this brief vignette is the focus on students' *doing*—thinking and expressing the results of thought. The teacher acted only as a coach. He helped the students mold their thinking skills and their habits of intellectual inquiry. Such skill training is the backbone of basic schooling. It proceeds one by one, each student gaining skill through critiqued experience. Schools that make it possible are effective schools.

T.R.S.

# 3
## Didactic Instruction

THE FORMS AND LEVELS OF DIDACTIC INSTRUCTION

THE BASIC PEDAGOGICAL precept of the Paideia Program is that all genuine learning arises from the activity of the learner's own mind. It may be assisted, guided, and stimulated by the activity of teachers. But no activity on the part of teachers can ever be a substitute and become the sole cause of a student's learning. When the activities performed by the teachers render students passive, the latter cease to be learners—memorizers, perhaps, but not learners.

Activity of mind is occasioned or initiated by wonder, sustained by interest and excitement, and reinforced by the pleasure inherent in the activity itself and by delight in its success. These are the things that teachers can do to assist and support the learning done by students who are actively engaged in that process.

Coaching for intellectual skills, both linguistic and mathematical, cannot be accomplished at all without activity on the part of the learners. They must perform under supervision, over and over again, to form the habit that constitutes any bodily or mental skill. Similarly, students who remain passive in seminar discussions are not participating; they might just as well be absent. Column Two and Column Three teaching, by the very nature of the learning they serve, readily conform to the pedagogical precept that all

47

genuine learning results from mental activity on the part of students.

Unfortunately, this is not true of Column One teaching. Didactic instruction, as it is usually conducted, tends much too frequently and regularly to violate the precept. The teacher's activity in talking to students and telling them what they should know may result in their remembering items of information, but it does not result in genuine knowledge, unless what is to be known is actively grasped by the mind rather than passively retained by the memory.

Consequently, the chief difficulty of didactic instruction is to make it the cause of active learning. To overcome that difficulty, it must first be noticed that there are two forms of didactic instruction and that they may be employed together or separately at the two levels of basic schooling.

Didactic instruction is either written or oral, addressed either to the eyes of readers or to the ears of listeners. Before the invention of printing, the ears were almost entirely the conduit of teaching. "Lecture," which means something read aloud, was the reading of a book (a scarce item) to a group of students. Now, with printed materials readily available, the two forms of didactic instruction can be related in a number of ways.

Some portion of what is to be known can be presented in written form—textbooks, manuals, or materials specially prepared by teachers for their students. Another portion can be communicated orally by the teacher in the classroom. This teaching may consist in the repetition of matters covered in writing; or it may consist in comments thereon; or it may deal with matters not to be found in the assigned readings. Any solution to the problem of how to make didactic instruction the cause of mental activity in students turns on a judicious combination of these two ways of didactic instruction.

The two levels of basic schooling are familiar to everyone. The lower level, whether it occupies the first six or first eight years, is the pre-departmental level. There the teacher should be engaged in all three kinds of teaching and be competent in all the basic subject-matters. The upper level is the departmental level. There the teachers are divided according to the subject-matters in which they are supposed to be particularly competent. There are English teachers, mathematics teachers, science teachers, history teachers, and so on.

For our present purposes, this difference between the two levels requires us to recognize that didactic teaching or telling may be more or less informal, may occupy more or less of the class time, may rely more or less on written materials. Only in the upper level should there be anything like a formal lecture that occupies the whole class period.

First, we may consider how to make didactic teaching effective at either level, overlooking their differences; then we will consider how the differences call for different measures to make it effective.

## READERS AND LISTENERS

If everything that is to be known by students about the subjects listed in Column One could be learned by the reading of written materials, there would be no need for teachers to talk or for students to listen. There would hardly be any need for schools. But not everything to be known can be learned from books, except by most remarkable students, such as those geniuses in history who have been entirely self-taught. Even those rare few would have to be taught how to read better than our young seem to be able to do.

The fundamental truth about reading as a means of learning is that it must be active, not passive. The reader must steadily ask himself or herself questions about what passes before his or her eyes and actively search for the answers. No such answers come without a close interpretation of the text, but such skill in reading seldom, if ever, exists in the twelve years of basic schooling, though it is the aim of basic schooling to start developing it.

This being so, didactic instruction must involve the oral presentation—teaching by telling, lecturing. But here too students must be active; they must think as they listen, just as they must think as they read. The best didactic teachers are those who manage to force their students to listen actively as well as to read actively. When students say that teacher so-and-so "makes the subject come alive," they really mean that he has somehow compelled *them* to come alive.

To be sure, some parts of every subject are hard to make interesting—the parts that are information and that precede organized knowledge. Bits of information, names and places in geography, terms and dates in history, spelling, etymology, and meanings of words in English or some other language, rules of grammatical construction, formulas and tables in science and mathematics— all these things must first be memorized: they acquire a *derived* interest only later, when integrated into knowledge.

Where the memorization of facts or items of information is the objective it is much better accomplished by written materials to be read than by oral presentations to be listened to. There is little need for explanation or for context. Teachers need only do what is necessary to motivate the memorizing by making clear why it is useful and predicting the interest it will lead to.

When we reach organized knowledge, the teacher's way of dealing with written materials changes. He turns from a drill master to a questioner; he makes use of quizzes. These are resorted to solely for the purpose of finding which students have failed to do the reading and for grading the accomplishment of those who have. Their primary purpose is to ensure that what has been read has been understood, not just learned by rote. But checking performance in this way is not the most important function performed by didactic teachers. Their greater role is oral instruction, which either supplements or goes beyond what students can learn by reading.

## INSTRUCTIVE SPEECH: TELLING AND LECTURING

For brevity's sake, let me enumerate without much comment the recommendations which, if followed, should increase the effectiveness of didactic instruction in oral form.

(a) To elicit active listening, the oral presentation must attract and sustain attention. It will succeed only if students expect questioning by the teacher both in the same class period as the lecture and in later periods. The subject matter is never "over and done with."

In a class period, not more than half the time should be devoted to telling, allowing at least the other half for asking. No class period will then turn into a session of passive, dreamy listening, or one in which students take notes in order to memorize what they think they will be expected to repeat on tests.

(b) Instructive speech must have a rhetorical as well as a logical dimension. Mere orderliness or even cogency will not suffice for effective didactic instruction. To be rhetorically effective in what they say, teachers must show their own lively interest in the subject as a whole by their "re-enactment" of the particular topic they are talking about. Enthusiasm and imaginative utterance are infectious. Listeners who need to be aroused are caught and made attentive. When teachers merely recite what they know and appear themselves bored by the recitation, their boredom too is contagious.

(c) Lively interest, the active mind, and steady attention are caused, in teachers and students both, by the emotions of wonder and discovery. Teachers should try to introduce some element of wonder at the beginning of their talk, and follow it by stirring up the excitement of discovery—discovery that requites the wonder. The wonder can be generated by presenting the lesson as a species of puzzle and the pleasure of discovery as an answer to the puzzle.

(d) Teachers who already know what students should come to know inevitably stand at some distance from their students. If, in their instructional talk, they remain at this distance, they will fail to reach the students. Again, if they attempt to bridge the gap by talking to students from the starting point of average ignorance, they will achieve little forward motion. They must aim instead at a point midway between their own knowledge and their students' ignorance.

Another way of wording this recommendation is to say that teachers must avoid two extremes: they must not talk over their students' heads—above their ability to grasp what is being said. And they must not talk down and lose their attention by being obvious, condescending, and dull. The middle ground consists in telling students things they can readily understand side by side with things they must make some effort to understand, that effort being re-enacted in the question period after the talk.

(e) The question-and-answer period that follows instructional speech in any class hour should always be two-way talk. It should involve questions asked by students and answered by teachers, as well as questions asked by teachers and answered by students.

Didactic teaching that is not accompanied by genuine conversation will always leave teachers in a state of ignorance about what, if anything, has been accomplished in the class hour. That lack of contact growing worse day after day will render any teaching less and less effective. Unless a teacher learns by question and answer what has happened to the minds of his listeners, he has no way of directing his own didactic effort.

(f) For maximum effectiveness, a classroom talk should begin by telling the listeners what they can expect to learn and why they should pay attention to it. The opening remarks should be uttered clearly and forcefully. The main body of the speech then follows the order outlined at the beginning, so that listeners perceive how one point leads to another. If the speech takes up three main points, each may be briefly summarized after being expounded. The speaker may need to repeat certain things. The presentation should close with a summary both brief and clear and leading to the question-and-answer session following.

The language of the presentation throughout should be clear and plain without being dull, and also elevated without being obscure. Teachers should not be afraid of being eloquent in their speech, or even dramatic in its delivery; and they should not resort to slang or vulgarisms in order to be popular. Changes of pace in delivery and in tone of voice will do much more to hold their audience; and if able, they can accompany their speech by gestures and other forms of body language. The best teachers are not afraid to regard themselves as actors on a stage.

(g) Last, and most important, is the recommendation that less is more. In any class hour devoted to didactic teaching, the aim is not to cover a predictable amount of ground, regardless of whether "covering" it leaves the students bewildered. The sensible aim is to cover as much as the students are able to absorb, as evidenced in the two-way talk that comes after the "lecturette." Less may be covered than was hoped for, but more will have been learned.

The seven recommendations set forth above apply primarily to instructional speech by teachers concerning matters not expounded in assigned readings. When readings are assigned, lecturing in the classroom should consist mainly of a brief but clearly organized summary (say, 15 minutes) detailing what the students should have learned from the books, followed by a longer session of questions and answers.

## DIDACTIC INSTRUCTION AT THE LOWER AND THE UPPER LEVELS

In the grades before the ability to read is sufficiently developed for acquiring either information or organized knowledge from print, talk is necessarily the sole means of didactic instruction. It should be simple, brief, and laced with questions as richly as possible, and as far removed as possible from formal lecturing.

As reading ability increases, didactic instruction combines written and oral presentations, relying on the written mainly for facts to be committed to memory and on the oral for explaining what knowledge is to be acquired.

At this lower level, didactic instruction will differ for different subject-matters. It will rely more on written materials for mathematics and science and more on teacher talk for history, geography, and the study of social institutions. In these grades didactic instruction concerning the English language, its grammar and syntax, should be closely integrated with the coaching of all the linguistic skills.

With respect to all the subjects studied at this level, classroom teachers are not expected to be experts. All that should be counted on is that they should know more than their students about the subjects studied and that they have facility—and even felicity—in communicating what they know. As always, the art of teaching is to hold and sustain attention, so as to give the pleasure of discovery and the delight of learning.

At the upper level, where departmental teachers are expected to have special competence in a field, students can also be expected to be competent readers. Consequently, a great deal of didactic instruction, especially in mathematics, science, and history, may take the written rather than the oral form, though never without being accompanied by two-way question-and-answer sessions. In no other way can the teacher make sure that students understand what they have read.

At this level, there should be in every school a small number of master teachers, at least one for every range of subjects. These teachers should be good lecturers, able to deliver effective didactic instruction about matters that are not adequately covered in books. If the size of the school prevents such teachers from reaching all students in a single classroom, closed-circuit television can be used to make their lectures serve the whole school.

Closed-circuit television can also be used in a school that lacks master teachers to present the best lectures available on a particular subject. When this device is resorted to, staff teachers should be present in the room to act as the best listeners and to impress and supplement the contents of the televised lecture by following it in the usual way with questions and answers.

M.J.A.

# PART TWO
# Subject Matters to Be Taught and Learned

# 4
## English Language and Literature

LANGUAGE, EVERYBODY'S BUSINESS

ACQUIRING LANGUAGE; improving one's ability to listen, speak, read, and write; achieving full literacy—these are the tasks of a lifetime. They are also indispensable for a fully human life, a lifetime in which learning never stops.

Beginning at home and in nursery school and continuing throughout basic schooling, parents and teachers can help to improve these abilities in every child and, by doing so, at the same time improve their own language skills. Good teachers are first of all good learners, who use their learning to teach better and their teaching to learn more.

Through the interactions of daily life, children learn how to listen and speak. They need little help to do so; they desperately want to speak. Helping them to read and write calls for more effort on the part of parents and teachers.

Very young children can learn to read if parents are willing to help them. Thousands of children are readers before going to school. There are advantages to learning to read at home, among them the student-teacher ratio of one-to-one, and the fact that parents are free—freer than most school teachers—to choose materials that interest the child they are teaching.

Language skills are unlikely to improve in a vacuum. Everything that is going on in a child's life can be used to further linguistic development. The best materials are those that provide children with interesting things to hear about, read about, talk about, and write about. The best coaching, whoever does it—teachers, parents, grandparents, siblings, other students—is done by people who are more concerned with helping a child understand what he reads and hears, to say what he wants to say, and to write what he wants to write, than with correcting every error.

## LANGUAGE AND LITERATURE IN A PAIDEIA SCHOOL

Three things characterize this part of the program.

The first is the presence of teachers who habitually practice language skills—chiefly reading and writing—and have an interest in improving them.

The second is a schedule that includes periods of intensive coaching and of weekly or bi-weekly seminars. Supervised practice in all the skills of language must be an integral part of all classes in a Paideia school. But special coaching sessions should, in addition, be scheduled throughout the week with the smallest student-teacher ratio obtainable. These should be frequent enough and long enough to yield progress, however small, in every session. That is the major reward for the often gruelling work of such sessions. They should continue at steadily advancing levels throughout all twelve years of Paideia schooling.

The third element in the Paideia Program is a list of readings, containing the best and most interesting examples of major kinds of writing.* The reading list is the backbone of a Paideia school. It contains (1) materials for the seminars, (2) readings for literature classes, and (3) supplementary texts to enrich the work done

---

*See the recommendations in the Appendix.

in other classes, which is to say that the list includes works of history, science, philosophy, and mathematics, as well as poems, stories, novels, plays, and other forms of imaginative literature.

The practice of coaching and the seminars set up in the earliest years of basic schooling will affect students' interests and abilities throughout the later years. Coaching to develop language skills should be supported by the work in other areas if what may seem like an impossibly demanding program is to be manageable by all students and not just the best. What junior and high school students can or cannot now do is no measure of what is possible in Paideia schooling.

COACHING TO IMPROVE THE LANGUAGE SKILLS

Language is an instrument for shaping, ordering, evaluating, and appreciating our thoughts and feelings. Language can organize them, clarify them, connect one with another, disjoin and reconnect them. Language does all this well or badly, depending on one's command of it.

Mastery in using and comprehending the words, the grammar, and the structures of a language is the first, but not the only goal of basic schooling. The second stage aims at the use of language to increase and consciously direct the powers of perception, reason, memory, imagination, judgment, and feeling. With this goal in mind coaching is kept from remaining a petty activity devoted to merely correcting mechanical errors.

Coaching lies at the heart of the language program. In the lower grades all teachers should be language coaches. In the upper grades, English teachers bear the major responsibility. Some coaching of language skills goes on in connection with all classroom discussions and written assignments, but the main instruments for the development and improvement of language and its use are the seminars and literature classes and scheduled coaching sessions.

The essence of coaching in matters of language is questioning: What do I mean? What does it say? Repeated questioning by teachers to correct errors and to strengthen performance will in time be internalized. Students should become so completely accustomed to the apt and suggestive process of questioning of what they have written or spoken that they form the habit of doing it by themselves to themselves for the rest of their lives.

To ensure the formation of such habits, coaching in all four language skills—listening, speaking, reading, and writing—should begin in the early years. Some time should be devoted to it every day for the entire twelve years, shorter and more frequent periods in the early years, longer and less frequent ones in the later years. Additional coaching must be available throughout the program for students who need it to keep from falling behind.

The particular skill that a teacher coaches at a particular time forms but a small part of a student's linguistic behavior. But the teacher's major aim is to help the student achieve adequacy in every aspect of language for every conceivable use. That is a tall order. Among the specific skills to be developed are:

*Speaking:* enunciation; pronunciation; memorization; diction (choice of words); phrasing; sentence structure; grammar; accuracy; fluency; how to ask and answer questions; how to describe a scene, explain a process, tell a story; how to argue, debate, discuss intelligently; how to make a speech.

*Listening:* memorization; how to recognize and understand different kinds of utterance; how to listen actively and accurately in conversation, discussion, argument; how to recognize the purpose of an utterance and to adapt one's thoughts to frame a relevant reply.

62

*Reading:* how to recognize and understand words, phrases, sentences, paragraphs, and other extended passages in prose, poetry, or drama; how to read different kinds of texts differently (stories, poems, novels, plays, expository prose); how to recognize the kind of writing that is being read; how to find what one wants in it without reading the whole; how to use reference books and do research.

*Writing:* penmanship; spelling, grammar, syntax, structure; diction; how to write a sentence, a paragraph, a letter, a story; how to explain a process; how to describe an object, person, scene; how to develop a thesis; how to revise a sentence, a paragraph, an entire composition; how to persuade and make writing memorable; how to translate from a foreign language; how to compose verse if one is so minded.

Teachers who have had experience in coaching language skills will recognize most of the suggestions that follow. It is important to keep in mind that in dealing with any linguistic performance however small (say, the pronunciation of a single word) or large (say, giving an oral or written report of research to an eleventh-grade class in American history), no language skill can be treated in isolation. A teacher who corrects or improves a passage or a spoken remark finds himself doing more, coaching in more than one skill, for language is a web whose parts alter with every change. This is a truth the language coach can take comfort in.

*Word study.* Linguistic competence begins with recognizing, understanding, and then remembering how to use words. It begins with speech. So the first thing to do in school might be to collect words. The teacher might write them on large cards in large, clear letters. Setting an example of good penmanship early is important. Then the field is open for every kind of discussion about words.

When words are put together in an utterance or a piece of writing, something new is created. The skill involved is that of making comprehensible and perhaps even beautiful compositions. Speaking and writing are performing arts and should be pleasingly presented.

The words a teacher chooses for even the youngest children should be big ones, big in the sense of important or interesting as well as written in large letters. Big, important words are better in the beginning than the usual lists of dull-looking, dull-sounding words that look alike and sound alike, and are more difficult for small children to remember because they are almost indistinguishable from one another. Instead of *cat, cot, bat, hat, ship, slip,* a teacher might try words like clover, pedestrian, barge, helicopter, ancestor, sibling, spruce, anger, refrigerator, delight. Indeed, a teacher is often well advised to have the children suggest the words. The ones they suggest will probably mean more to them and therefore be more productive of learning. Teachers and children can do many things with words: connect them with connectors, attach them to verbs, detach and reattach them, put them in sentences or stories with other words, rhyme them, or even abandon them when they cease to be interesting.

What the children do with words may not seem at the time to have accomplished much. But they will have pronounced them, read them, remembered some of them, spelled them, talked about them. The next step is to write them. Older children can continue collecting words, in lists, on cards, in notebooks. They should as soon as possible begin to use a dictionary for pronunciation, spelling, definitions, and contexts. Interest in words thus begun should be sustained throughout basic schooling in ways appropriate to the interests and development of the students.

*Speaking and listening.* Going back to the early years, practice in speaking and listening, while not more important than practice in reading and writing, is nevertheless crucial. Practice gives the

64

confidence necessary for speaking in a group, a skill that is essential to the conditions of learning in school. Practice in speaking can take many forms, but it should also inculcate the attitudes, habits, and good manners necessary for conversation, half of which is the art of listening. Teachers in the early grades might try engaging every child in true conversation for a few minutes every day.

*Reading.* The early years are also crucial in making or breaking the habit of reading. Early reading exercises should always be enjoyable and reward the child's effort with the pleasure of learning new things, of being excited by a story, of arousing curiosity about people, places, and things. Too often boring materials discourage children from the necessary effort of reading. Word drills may be necessary but should not be passed off as reading.

In the early as in the later years, reading is far more complex than recognizing and attaching meaning to one word after another; it entails a grasp of context and intention. What kind of book is it? What am I hoping to get from it? What will it demand of me? These legitimate questions apply at any stage.

Reading is a major source of information and knowledge and promotes the understanding of ideas. But its benefits barely begin there. Reading offers sustenance for the spirit as well as the mind, and for the youngest human beings as well as for the older ones. All should learn early that a reader, besides being informed, may be transported, enriched, beguiled, delighted, amused, consoled, ennobled; taken to new and wonderful places, some of which are pure invention; introduced to characters who may become life-long companions; allowed to overhear conversations that say what no one has ever said before; invited to share feelings that deepen their own. And the pleasures of reading are always enhanced by talking about what one has read.

*Writing.* Writing in the early years may well begin with the possession of a notebook, the sole purpose of which is for each child to record his thoughts and observations. Every pupil might be encouraged to keep a journal for some months at least.

Dictation and comprehension exercises in the early years provide practice in spelling, punctuation, and the ability to connect the written with the spoken word. They exercise the skills of listening and remembering and also offer models of good speech.

The task of revising one's writing should begin as early as possible and should be aided by the student's reading aloud what he or she has written. Listening to one's prose helps develop an ear for language. Mistakes and weak spots that pass unnoticed in silent reading will strike—and shock—the ear.

From about the age of 9 or 10, as students' abilities mature and the seminars become more formal, they and the preparation for them afford a good opportunity for coaching language skills. Writing assignments are geared to preparation for seminar discussions or to a backward look upon them.

As the knowledge and reading skill of the students grows more complex, writing also grows important as a means of learning. Coaching writing in the later years of schooling aims at helping students to learn how to think, to give full expression to what they feel, and to organize what they know. The teacher becomes a discerning and respectful editor, keeping a balance between preserving accepted standards of good writing on the one hand, and encouraging the growth of student's originality on the other. Standards of good writing are well established, but not absolute.

To conclude: Teachers engaged in coaching the language skills should emulate the ways successfully used in coaching other kinds of performances—acting, singing, ballet, rowing, swimming, or tennis. This piece of advice suggests also that coaching sessions ought to begin with a warming up exercise. Writing can be a warm-up for discussion, reading a warm-up for writing, talking a warm-up for either writing or discussion. Warm-ups marshal the mental resources.

Next comes the performance. It should always be followed by a critique, consisting in an array of both its good and bad points; and this in turn should lead to a second performance, one that tries to correct the weaknesses and to build on the strengths, the second try ending on a positive note by an explicit recognition of the effort and the particulars of what still needs to be done.

But remember: no method or technique will work unless interesting materials are used. Nothing can replace interest—the desire to know. Language must be seen as a means to fulfill that desire.

## DIDACTIC INSTRUCTION IN LANGUAGE AND LITERATURE

Didactic instruction—giving information or offering explanations—is reserved for the upper grades, when students beyond the age of 11 or 12 have acquired sufficient experience and knowledge of language and literature to be interested in them as subjects themselves.

Didactic instruction in language focuses on structures. In literature, it focuses on the history of literature and on the principles underlying its appreciation and criticism.

The English language as a subject matter includes its grammar, semantics, etymology, and history. Didactic instruction in literature treats the forms and genres of literature, their structure, historical and biographical contexts, as well as relation to past and present works in art, history, science, technology, philosophy, mathematics, and literature itself. This part of the program is intended to provide information that will enhance the understanding and appreciation of what is read in seminars and in literature classes.

## THE DISCUSSION OF LITERATURE IN ENGLISH CLASSES

It is not enough to know how to read a word, a page, or a book; full literacy requires familiarity with different kinds of writing and the ability to read them in the way that is appropriate to each kind.

The acquisition of this power can only begin in school. Literacy—like musicianship—will continue to grow long after schooling has ended. The Paideia Program does not ask that students read everything in school. It does require them to read adequately enough examples of different kinds of writing so as to be able to read without guidance anything they want to read. The aim is to instill the habit of reading for information, for knowledge, for understanding, and for pleasure.

In traditional schools, literature usually means stories, poems, essays, novels, and plays written in English. The Paideia list of recommended readings includes examples of these genres as material for seminars and literature classes, most of the works being in English. But works of history, philosophy, science, and mathematics also form part of the list, many of them translations from other languages. As a group these writings deserve to be called important, beautiful, difficult, and profound. As long as they are interesting and informative, as long as they arouse and help satisfy the curiosity of young people, the teacher's choice of things to be read is less important than the purpose for which they are read, which is to advance literacy.

To fulfill that purpose, different kinds of works should be read in every year of schooling. Some will be used in seminars only; some will be read and discussed in literature classes; others will warrant treatment in both places. Literature classes will occasionally serve as a place of rehearsal for the more exacting seminar. Whatever choices are made for any type of treatment, the readings must be discussed and the discussion must involve students and teachers in lively, mutual questioning and responding. Only active participation fosters learning and mental growth.*

The role of the English teacher or seminar leader is to help make different kinds of books accessible, intelligible, memorable. This may require some reading aloud from part of the text; some *explication de texte* or "close reading" of difficult passages; some practice in reading a certain kind of book very quickly and others very slowly; some reading of only parts of long and difficult works as the Paideia reading list suggests; but never destroying the integrity of imaginative works by reading less than the whole.

The first thing teachers should do in assigning a new reading is to introduce the work as a certain kind of story; or as a document that helped persuade a people to rebel; or as an initial report of a scientific discovery or of a theory that revolutionized science or mathematics; or as an example of the most moving and beautiful sonnets in the English language. The teacher is free to spur interest by adding something about the life and achievement of the author.

Keeping this kind of didactic instruction to a minimum will put the emphasis where it belongs—on the experience of reading the text. Helping to shape that experience is all that teaching literature can do. The texts vary in character and complexity, but the methods are always basically the same, for children and for adults.

## DISTINCTIVE FEATURES OF ENGLISH INSTRUCTION IN THE PAIDEIA PROGRAM

The traditional role of English teachers in the upper grades after departmentalization differs from what has been described in these pages. Under the Paideia proposal, all teachers are responsible for

*See Chapter 1 on the conduct of seminars.

supervising the right use of language skills, but the teachers of English bear the major responsibility, and in the upper grades they coach in *all* the skills of language, not just the writing of compositions.

At the same time, they are also teachers of literature and leaders of seminars. They are not the only seminar leaders; all upper grade teachers are expected to participate. Teachers of English lecture and discuss language and literature as themselves objects of study, awakening young people to the aesthetic, emotional, and intellectual experiences to be derived from poetry and other forms of fiction

Paideia graduates should be able to read, without help and with appropriate care and attention, almost any text in modern English. They should be able to use the English language easily in speaking or writing on most occasions. And they should be able to judge what they hear and read by reference to its purpose, its adherence to appropriate means, and even by standards of truth.

These goals may seem to many unreachable, even if they are desirable. We think that they are without question desirable. We also think they are reachable, and not just for a chosen few, but for every American child. The answer to the doubters is that all children are brilliant enough to learn and speak their native language. The trouble later on is not that some children cannot learn to read and write because they have low I.Q.'s, but rather that these children have low I.Q.'s because they have not been taught to read and write well enough. Literacy, the acquisition of knowledge, and the ability to think are interdependent. Everyone knows this, but the Paideia Program believes it strongly enough to propose acting on the belief.

G.V.D.

# 5
# Mathematics

## WHY MATHEMATICS SHOULD BE EXTENSIVELY STUDIED

THE STUDY of the exact sciences in general, and in particular of the mathematics on which they are increasingly based, supplies the mind with certain nutrients. Other disciplines, such as languages, literature, or history, do not provide these same nutrients, at least to the same degree. They provide other nutrients that the exact sciences, just because they *are* exact, do not provide. Raw experience does not provide these nutrients at all.

The nutrients supplied by the study of mathematics consist of certain properties that give mathematics its essential character. As these properties are encountered by students, understood through the solution of concrete problems, and ultimately *felt* as a kind of intellectual presence, young minds enlarge and experience a higher degree of freedom. This process was described by Plato long ago.

Among the properties of mathematics that enable it to have this effect on the mind are: order, rigor, logical development from simple to complex, exactness, universality, abstraction, economy, and elegance (symmetry, diversity, rhythm, balance). To these general properties we can add certain operational tools that are most beautifully employed in mathematics but that are also applicable to systematic thought in general. Among these tools are the ideas of symbol, of function, of transformation, and the fundamental idea of proof.

An educated person should understand the nature of a mathematical proof, and the difference between a mathematical proof and a proof beyond a reasonable doubt, as in a court of law. This distinction is crucial for understanding many other things that are important in the world today.

Behind the idea of a mathematical proof lies the even more basic idea of an axiomatic system. A mathematical proof is characterized by the fact that a conclusion *follows* from the premises or assumptions. In an axiomatic system, we may assume whatever we please, as long as our assumptions do not contradict one another; but we are then restricted by the laws of thought to certain conclusions. Any other conclusions are illegitimate.

It is perhaps this characteristic of legitimacy that underlies the great satisfactions to be derived from mathematics. Many students speak of the intense pleasure that is gained from the certainty of mathematical results. In most things that we study, as well as in life itself, there are no certainties. An answer to a mathematical question, however, the solution of a mathematical problem, is either right or wrong—period. Furthermore, to the extent that the problem has roots in reality, reality has thus been ordered, understood, controlled. It gives human beings great pleasure to do this, as it should, for it is one of the fundamentally human things to do.

Beyond all this, an esthetic satisfaction derives from using the mind successfully in a field from which vagueness, inexactness, subjectivity, and emotion are banished. The experience parallels that produced by reading a play of Shakespeare's or contemplating a painting by Botticelli. The latter example is particularly apt. Mathematics, in its dealings with the world, isolates certain elements (the assumptions) and arranges and rearranges them in

72

order to produce an ordered and coherent whole that both makes independent sense and throws light upon the world of which it is in some sense an imitation. Is that not what Botticelli did, too?

## THE WAYS OF TEACHING MATHEMATICS

In a Paideia school, all students study mathematics for the entire twelve years of basic schooling. Actually, it is expected that children in the first grade will have had some prior exposure to mathematical ideas, if only through playing games that involve or are based on numbers. Thereafter, no week passes, and probably no day, in which all students do not do some mathematics.

As with most of the other disciplines in the Paideia curriculum, mathematics is dealt with in all three Columns of learning. The didactic teaching of the concepts, operations and uses of mathematics is a leading activity of Column One classes. Coaching mathematical skills is one of the most important activities in Column Two work groups. Discussions of the significance, utility, and delight of mathematics belong to the Column Three seminars.

*First Column Mathematics: didactic teaching.* For the first few years of basic schooling, all the teachers in a Paideia school are teachers of mathematics, and they are expected to teach the subject to all of their students. Similarly, during the first few years of basic schooling all teachers are teachers of language, of history and of other subjects as well. Arithmetical operations, at least, are involved in the discussion of almost all subjects in a school, and teachers of language arts, of science or history, even of art or music, should not avoid them, but rather take every opportunity to reinforce simple mathematical ideas.

Those who teach mathematics in the lower grades will meet with practically every student practically every day. Teaching very young children arithmetic is both a challenge and a pleasure. They are

73

quick to learn if the subject is presented to them in the right way. This means doing a little at a time, keeping the classes amusing, and making sure that no one falls irretrievably behind the others.

There are certain general rules of good mathematics teaching that apply throughout the years of basic schooling, but that are particularly important during the first few. The first of these rules has to do with the approach to a new subject. Many adults prefer to have the rules of a new subject explained to them first, after which they expect to be able to apply the rules—if they can remember them. But even with adults this logical way may not work well; with younger minds it is pedagogically ineffective. Far better is to begin by presenting a number of new facts and then letting the novices try to intuit the rules that organize them.

Of course, a good teacher does not allow his pupils to flounder for any considerable length of time; the children may or may not be able to discover the rules by themselves. A hint here, a suggestion there, may be required to direct the students toward the goal. But it is wise to be chary of such help. The best teachers ask many more questions than they answer; ideally, perhaps, a teacher should never answer a direct question from a student, but instead respond by asking another question that will aid the student to solve his own problem. At any rate, keep the main point in mind. Provide the students with a relatively large mass of facts to begin with—problems, examples, diagrams on the blackboard (in the case of geometry)—and let them try to figure out why things are as they are. What they learn on their own they will not forget; what they are told they are likely to forget quickly.

Another general rule, applicable throughout the years of basic schooling, is to remember that the mathematics that is taught at this level has many connections with the real world. Mathematics is a complex structure of pure thought that nevertheless is rooted in the most practical human concerns. Good teachers do not ignore this or allow their students to forget it. This caution should be borne in mind when assigning problems. Those in the text-books are often left undone because they are silly, foolish, or ir-relevant.

To be sure, mathematics also has a meaning that is not practi-cal and down-to-earth. Mathematics may have its feet on the ground, but it has its head in the clouds. The great thing about it is in fact the movement up and down and down and up.

It would be hard to lay too much stress on the rule that no stu-dent should be allowed to fail totally and fall behind his or her fellow students. In learning English, a tiny child can afford to miss the meaning of a word or one rule of grammar, because his con-stant practice of speaking and reading the language will eventu-ally bring it to his attention again. Not so with the rules of arith-metic, or with the multiplication table. And once the class has moved on to algebra the neglected rule, which may not be used again for a long time, will prove a stumbling block: an essential connector of the great house of cards that is mathematics will be lacking, and the house will be in danger of tumbling down around the student's ears.

For this reason, passage through the course of mathematics in a Paideia school is not a straight line pointing or slanting upward, but instead a rising and dipping spiral; the general direction is upward, but the line often dips down as well, as subjects are re-turned to and old concepts, operations, and results are reviewed for use over and over again.

A last general point: bad textbooks and other teaching mate-rials, in mathematics as elsewhere in the Paideia curriculum, are probably worse than none. Some of the best mathematics teach-ers use no textbooks; this is hard work, but it pays off. Textbooks generally answer too many questions too quickly and thereby *slow down* possible progress.

*Second Column coaching of mathematics skills.* The importance of not letting any students fall too far behind has been emphasized. There are various ways to do this, and they all take work, but it must be done if the goal is to be achieved. One way is to assign a lot of homework in the form of examples and problems, and then make sure the work is completed. This means reading and marking homework and handing it back with annotations, and discussing it with students afterwards as needed.*

Another way is to take the time to do problems in class and involve all students in their solution. Here, the abler students should not be permitted to solve all the problems, even if that is easier for the teacher. Balance must be maintained between abandoning some slower students and boring the quicker ones. To cope with the predicament, the abler students may be given more difficult problems so that all are working together but not at the same tasks. At other times, the abler students can be asked to help the others to solve problems and understand concepts. If not overdone, this is an effective pedagogical method which takes care of all students at once, slow and fast alike.

It is, of course, a general rule of all good teaching that no student should be allowed to remain silent through a class period; this is especially important in mathematics, where a look of vague interest on a student's face can mask utter bewilderment or confusion.

*Computers as mathematics coaches.* Computers make acceptable coaches of mathematics, for they naturally possess many of the characteristics that make for good coaching. They are patient; they never tire if you keep asking them foolish questions. They are not driven by the human compulsion to announce rules too soon, that is, before the student has found them by himself. They

---

*Older students may be counted on to help younger students with their homework; if this help does not come about spontaneously, arrangements can be made to provide it.

can be easily programmed to offer an almost unlimited number of problems to solve, which is the best kind of mathematics practice. And they are never tempted to humiliate a careless or ignorant student in front of his fellows. If computers take over some of the coaching in mathematics, at all levels of the curriculum, this will allow the human instructors to concentrate on the things they do best, among which is relating mathematics to the world in which human beings, not computers, live.

It need hardly be pointed out that some instructional computer games are an excellent way to practice mathematical skills. Such games can be used to teach young children important algorithms, the multiplication table, and the squares of numbers up to 25 or beyond. Games are also useful for older students in conveying concepts in geometry, trigonometry, and algebra.

*Mathematics in the Third Column of learning.* Seminars and discussions undergo major changes as the students move through the course of basic schooling. In the earlier years, Third Column activities are generally informal and often unscheduled; a teacher may simply decide to sit down with his or her pupils and discuss an idea or result that has emerged from a session of didactic teaching or coaching. Later, scheduled discussions of the mathematics books on the Paideia reading list (see Appendix) may be formally scheduled.

Yet mathematical formulas, rules, algorithms, problems, and the like probably will never be discussed in seminars. It is mathematics as a human endeavor, as described by mathematicians who have written about doing it or about its applications to the world, that can constitute especially interesting subjects for treatment in Third Column seminars. The relation of mathematics to other fields, such as the exact sciences or music, can also be dealt with there.

Questions about what mathematics is, from the most general

point of view, can also be broached in seminars. For example, the question of why, if not the question of whether, mathematics should be studied throughout the twelve years of basic schooling might make for a lively discussion. Both students and teachers might learn from each other, which is what the Third Column of teaching and learning is intended to bring about.


MATHEMATICS IN THE PAIDEIA CURRICULUM

Departmental instruction in the mathematics part of the curriculum probably should not begin before the seventh or eighth grade. By that time, however, all students should have become comfortable with mathematics through their constant, pervasive, and rewarding exposure to it during the preceding years. In the upper half of basic schooling, when mathematical subjects are taught didactically in formal classes, these classes should be grouped by ability rather than by age or grade level. The amount of a given subject covered may differ for less able classes than for more able ones. But all classes, regardless of ability, study the same subjects—from arithmetic to calculus and beyond.

The main subjects are as follows:

> Arithmetic
> Algebra
> Geometry
> Differential and integral calculus
> Statistics; probabilistic mathematics
> Computers
> The history of mathematics
> The relation of mathematics to other fields

*Arithmetic.* Arithmetic is the basic mathematical science and for that reason is tremendously important. Arithmetic is used by practically everybody every day of their lives. Our society, like any reasonably complex human society, functions with the aid of deeply ingrained mathematical elements and tools. Not to know how to use at least the most elementary of these is to lead a second-class life.

Accordingly, students should study arithmetic for the entire twelve years of basic schooling. That is, they should constantly return to it, using the skills they have already mastered, perhaps years before, to new problems and situations.

*Algebra.* Here the fact that mathematics is a language causes difficulties for many students. It is as hard to learn algebraic notations for mental operations one has been performing with ease all along as it is to learn the grammar of the language one has been speaking correctly for years. Elementary algebra crosses the chasm between the arithmetic of everyday life and the abstract symbolism of mathematics proper. The use of symbols here gives the young students a concrete illustration of the power of abstraction. The ability to think abstractly lies at the root of the ability to think at all.

Intermediate algebra introduces important new concepts. In the equation $y = ax^2 + bx + c$, the *a, b,* and *c*, on the one hand, and the $x$ and $y$, on the other, represent two different kinds of unknown quantities. The *a, b,* and *c*, which are constants, can be any quantity, but once they are assigned values they do not change. Then $x$ is allowed to vary, which results in different values for $y$. The value of $y$ is then said to be a function of the value of $x$. Getting this straight gives joy to many students.

The higher algebra of sets, groups, rings, and the like should be studied toward the end of the course, though the concept of a set can be introduced earlier. Boolean algebra and elementary symbolic logic should be introduced to all students toward the end of the twelve years.

*Geometry.* The ancients studied geometry, they said, because of its utility. But plane geometry is more than just a very useful science; it is also beautiful, and possesses a profound logical rightness. Particularly as presented by Euclid in his *Elements,* plane geometry is a superb example of an axiomatic system. Ideally, the best mathematics teacher in the school should teach the first year of geometry to all the children. The beauty and rigor of plane geometry escapes many educators and even some mathematicians, who are proposing that the subject be dropped from the U.S. curriculum. This would be a tragic error.

The modern world may well have come into being on the day when the French mathematician Descartes devised *analytical geometry,* a combination of plane geometry, elementary algebra, and arithmetic. It logically follows them in the curriculum. It should also include *trigonometry,* something that, in its geometric context, should be covered in no more than one or two class sessions, and thereafter made use of in conjunction with a hand-held calculator.

Descartes' idea—that it is possible to attach a unique pair of numbers to every distinct point on the Euclidean plane—is so simple and at the same time so fraught with consequences that it makes one dizzy to think of them. A cannon might be shot off in the schoolyard every time the idea is presented to a new class: it is important enough for a royal salute.

And toward the end of the basic course, all students should be at least introduced to that beautiful construction of pure mind: projective geometry.

*Differential and integral calculus.* One studies calculus not because one will necessarily use it—most people do not—but because its bedrock utility has a beauty of its own. It came to be as follows. Descartes, at the beginning of the seventeenth century, had invented analytical geometry, which reduced the points on the plane to numbers, making them easier to manipulate. But the points in analytical geometry are all at rest. Most of the points in the real world, like projectiles and planets and photons, are moving, often very fast. A new device, calculus, had to be invented, and it was, half a century after Descartes, by the Englishman Newton and the German Leibniz, in order to deal with moving points and changing situations.

At first their calculus was a crude instrument. The problem was that one of the most fundamental mathematical concepts, that of *limit,* had not been well defined, though it lay at the heart of the calculus. It was not until the nineteenth century that this was understood. Learning about limits is one of the most interesting parts of studying calculus, and it is of importance in other areas as well.

For example, the concept of limit can be employed to "invent" the exponential function $e^x$ and its variant $e^{ix}$ (where $i$ is the square root of minus one—in itself an evocative concept). This has the fruitful result of removing the mystery from logarithms, trigonometric functions, and their derivatives, and so makes available to students what may be the most powerful mathematical idea ever developed. Let the instructor be reassured: the whole idea can be learned in a few class sessions, and it is remarkably effective; among other things, it is the heart of the hand-held calculator.

*Statistics; probabilistic mathematics.* The study of statistics teaches one to distrust statistics, as well as election polls, economic charts, the prophecies of stock brokers, and the like. It also introduces students to a wonderful set of facts about the behavior of things in aggregates, or large groups. There are, for example, striking mathematical similarities among the range of reading skills, the shape of a pile of sand, and the form of a butterfly's wings.

To grasp this helps students to understand statistical methods. It is imprudent to try to get through life, in our age, without this understanding.

Statistics is a branch, and a relatively minor one, of a large and important division of mathematics: *probabilistic mathematics*. It was pointed out earlier that students, especially young ones, take great pleasure in the exactitude of mathematical results and in the solution of precise, deterministic problems. But mathematics, particularly the kind of mathematics that is done today, is also capable of dealing with probability situations. This is at least as fundamental as the consideration of exact relationships, and perhaps even more widely applicable to the real world when mathematics deals with it. So, toward the end of the twelve-year course, the nature of probability theory should be presented to all students in a fashion similar to that employed for exact mathematical relationships. Simple lessons and exercises in probability can, in fact, be introduced in the first few grades, starting with the toss of a coin and guessing heads or tails.

*Computers.* Mathematics both is and is not a language like a natural language. Natural languages are employed by human beings to communicate with one another; they use conventional symbols, both spoken and written, to convey messages—information and knowledge. Mathematics employs symbols that stand for odd kinds of things (entities that are somehow both more and less real than ordinary things) but usually not primarily for communication. Instead, mathematics is a device for expressing certain kinds of truth that cannot be expressed in ordinary language or any other way but its own.

The languages with which we address and command computers are much more like natural languages; we would not be able to communicate with computers without them. Is that important? Yes, already it is hardly imaginable that we could ever again live without computers, and this will become inconceivable with the next generation of computers.

Computer languages possess two qualities that are instructive. On the one hand, they are like the languages we use to speak to dogs. In speaking to a dog one must above all be consistent, always employ the same tone to express the same command, never become impatient but instead recognize that if the dog does not understand, it is one's own fault, not the dog's. So it is with computers. On the other hand, addressing a computer is like addressing a powerful tyrant, toward whom we must also be careful to express ourselves in the right way lest we be misunderstood—the penalty for which can be very serious. If a tyrant expects to be addressed in a certain way (for example, on one's knees), he is not likely to smile if one speaks to him standing up and tries to explain the fact by saying that at home one does not kneel to tyrants. He will hand you your head. Computers, too, will hand you your head if you address them in the wrong way, that is, in a way to which they are not accustomed.

*The history of mathematics.* In the preceding pages it was impossible to avoid discussing the history of mathematics when describing various mathematical subjects. Mathematical history should be taught throughout basic schooling—and mathematical biography as well. Failure to do so makes mathematics inhuman; doing it as may be appropriate along the way reminds all students that mathematics is one of the great human achievements and a continuing adventure. Nor should mathematics teachers be the only ones to be informative about the history of mathematics. History teachers should do the same also.

*The relation of mathematics to other fields.* All the exact sciences, and to a lesser degree all the social sciences, employ mathematics and can no longer be taught without it. But mathematics works differently in different sciences; not only are different skills used, but they are used in different ways. From time to time, as various branches of mathematics are studied and various skills are learned, the utility of a given type of mathematics to a given science should be discussed.

Curiously, this is also interesting in the case of music, an art and not a science at all. Music is sounding mathematics, as it was once said, and mathematics silent music. The two disciplines seem in some strange way, very hard to define, to reflect each other. All American youngsters are interested in, not to say fascinated by, music; to show them its intimate connections with mathematics may serve to recommend mathematics to them. Perhaps, in a Paideia school, the recommendation would go the other way.

## THE PLACE OF MATHEMATICS IN A PAIDEIA SCHOOL

Mathematics is everywhere in the Paideia curriculum and in a Paideia school. All students study mathematics for all of the twelve years of basic schooling. The benefits of this total immersion approach to the teaching of mathematics are fundamental for girls as well as for boys, for those less apt as well as for those more apt.

Paideia graduates will have studied mathematics in Column One classes in which they are introduced to the ideas, operations, and uses of mathematics. They will have spent hundreds of hours being coached, in Column Two work groups, in mathematical skills. They will have discussed and will have begun to comprehend basic mathematical ideas in Column Three seminars. They will leave a Paideia school reasonably competent in mathematics, of which they will also be unafraid. Hardly anything could be more important for young people in the world of today, and of tomorrow.

It hardly needs to be pointed out that mathematical competence possessed by Paideia graduates will stand them in good stead. Not long ago, many jobs were available that required little or no knowledge of and skill in mathematics. Today, the number of such jobs is dwindling. In the future, the great majority of jobs will be in the so-called information industries, or will demand information skills. Mathematics is central to the manipulation and dissemination of information. Mathematical illiterates will be left behind.

In addition, mathematical reasoning is one of the most human things that human beings do. It is a native ability, but if mathematics is not studied, and studied early, the ability can atrophy, or at least remain largely undeveloped. Mathematics is also enormously satisfying, and not to be able to engage in it—for work or for play—is to be deprived of one of the highest and most innocent pleasures that human beings can enjoy. It is a sad commentary on basic schooling as it now exists that most children do not know this, nor would they believe it if they were told.

C.V.D.

# 6
# Science

SCIENCE is a search for a rational explanation of natural phenomena. It is a continuing activity. Though it accumulates a body of knowledge that is interconnected and self-consistent and is, therefore, useful in the practical world, its fundamental action is search. Its extended action is application.

*Pure science* aims at gaining knowledge of the structures and operations of the elements of the universe, without regard to the possible usefulness of the knowledge. The search is directed at achieving truths which are clearly demonstrable to all men. The result is satisfying in itself. The fact that such knowledge can be beneficial to mankind, however, is often a strong additional stimulus to the search.

*Applied science* takes what pure science discovers and arranges for its utility, adapting it technically and economically, with the results we call inventions. Engineering is applied science, and so is the practice of medicine.

*Technology* covers the operation and maintenance of the devices developed by applied science, as well as the complicated processes of manufacture. These now generally derive from applied science. Formerly, invention and technology usually came first by inspired manipulation such as that of Thomas Edison, and the devices so made spurred theoretical minds to find out why they worked. Now the regular, established practice of scientific research has reversed the roles.

The obligation of basic schooling is to provide an introduction to the scientific mode of thinking as exemplified in *pure science.* Such an introduction must be of sufficient depth and breadth to allow a person thus prepared to pursue advanced study at any of the levels of scientific activity in keeping with one's desire and ability. More important still, this introduction provides an understanding of science that contributes to the maturing of the mind. Science is an integral part of the unique activities of human beings.

Of the many different branches of natural science, some are subdivisions of a more general category: for example, botany, zoology, entomology and ornithology are specialized parts of biology. Some sciences are closely associated with other sciences as astronomy is with physics, or geology, which draws on physics, chemistry, and biology.

The last three named—physics, chemistry, and biology—may be considered the sciences underlying all others, and hence form a central concern of basic schooling. All, of course, make extensive use of mathematics.

GOALS FOR THE TEACHING OF SCIENCE

Instruction in science in a Paideia school runs through all twelve years, even though science in the early grades is not a separate subject. The elementary teacher must establish in the minds of the young the conditions for understanding science and therefore needs to be aware of the ends toward which the science curriculum is directed.

During the course of schooling, every student should gain a reasonable understanding of (1) the scientific mode of thought;

87

(2) the present conception of the physical universe; (3) the nature of living systems generally and of man in particular; and (4) the development of scientific thought in the past and its implications for the future.

These four points by no means constitute a course outline. Rather, they represent a residue of what should remain from the long-term experience of science in the school. The curriculum should show how scientific thinking enters into almost every kind of human activity. If students are to attain this awareness, they must be led to develop certain attitudes characteristic of science. The scientific mode of knowing is distinguished by being objective, general, quantified, and theoretical.

It is *objective* in being freed from personal idiosyncrasies. The need for scientific fact to be demonstrable to all persons anywhere and at any time underlies scientific method. It follows that scientific operations and the conclusions or generalizations drawn from them must be stated in simple and unambiguous language.

It is *general* in that the knowledge pertains to whole classes of subjects, even though what may be observed is individual and particular. The power of the abstracting process allows the mind to focus on one quality at a time and to abstract the common properties of objects that share that given quality, regardless of many other ways in which those objects differ.

It is *quantified* in making use of measurements abstracted from direct apprehension and their generalized representations, yet representing the wholeness of the thing observed. The powers of mathematics can be trained on the properties of an object only when these can be measured.

It is *theoretical* in seeking always to establish relationships between observed facts (and their theories), thus permitting prediction of future behavior. For instance, so simple a theoretical statement as $E = mc^2$ indicates a relation between matter and en-

88

ergy. A wave equation converts knowledge of a present state into knowledge of a future probability.

Scientific knowledge results from an accumulation of observations, reflections, generalizations, and judgments. The pedagogy of science consists in advancing young persons from the kind of thinking they spontaneously perform—differentiation, comparison, generalization (usually untested), perception of sequence, rough estimation of amounts and of chances, and similar efforts to orient themselves in the world—to a more rigorous understanding that will introduce the scientific outlook into their everyday thinking.

This "rigorous understanding" depends on: the *facts;* the *theories* developed to explain them logically and comprehensively; and the *testing* of these theories.

The fact, established by observation and experiment, is the ultimate unit of science. A fact is a phenomenon, a thing or event known through the senses. It must be reproducible within the range of uncertainty dictated by the apparatus and the observation or measurement to be performed. Anecdotes about events that cannot be reproduced cannot become a part of science.

The theories developed from the reproducible facts must be logical and consistent with accepted scientific laws. Theory may be understood as a linking up of a set of facts in a unified picture, in which cause and effect or probabilistic relations obtain, and by which one may accurately predict results within a defined experimental situation.

The testing is done by comparing actual measurements with the prediction made when the theory is applied. It must fit not only the set of facts for which it was designed, but also all the situations where it might reasonably be applied. A theory that fails such a test must be modified or discarded and a new one sought.

The great underlying idea of science as it studies the universe is the assumption that the entire world of nature is an arena in which logical and mutually consistent laws continuously function. This assumption, however, is made with the qualifying thought that precision in any measurement is limited both by the finiteness of human abilities and by certain indeterminacies in nature itself. But these too can be studied experimentally and defined.


## THE TEACHING OF SCIENCE

The successful teaching of science, like that of other subjects, depends upon a sympathetic and adequately prepared teacher. In the early and middle grades adequate preparation does not require special competence in the details of science; what it does require is a clear understanding of the nature of science and of the value of scientific thinking. The preceding pages of this chapter should be thoroughly understood and their message should become familiar ideas in the mind of such a teacher.

School teaching has tended to present science as dealing with a set of phenomena apart from ordinary life, a matter of lore to be memorized like the names of plants in a forest. A burning candle sealed in a glass jar will go out, for example, as all students can see and remember. But this fact is not something to treasure up by itself. It must be related to other facts and principles in a framework which *is* science and which permits reasoning about other phenomena throughout the universe.

The snuffed-out candle, in short, constitutes the beginning of a mental process, not its end. How long does it burn if the glass jar has twice the volume? Or if two candles are used? If the sealed jar with the candle is placed on a balanced scale, does the balance change from before to after burning? Is anything in the jar used up? Is anything new produced? How has the mind of man come to answer such questions? It is the way of thinking that is science, not the information alone.

To repeat, the teacher's feeling of comfort and familiarity with this way of thinking must be well developed. Spontaneity, improvised comments and questions can then enliven the class sessions and make the subject into a lively, ever-new challenge to the students, especially as they come to realize the wide range of methods and devices that exist for solving the problems that a simple experiment can suggest.

## SCIENCE IN THE EARLY YEARS

Since science is not a specific subject in the early years (K through 3), an indirect preparation for the later work must take place; the ground must be laid for formal instruction in science from the fourth grade on. Scientists generally believe that an understanding of the physical comes first through imagination, in movie-like fashion. An image presents itself to the mind and from it the intellect constructs a model, instinctively following the principles of completeness and consistency. A "model" is useful in scientific thought because in dealing with complicated phenomena the human mind more effectively handles organized schemes or pictorial scenarios than abstract conceptions.

If the observed facts prove inconsistent with the workings of the imagined model, then the model must be altered or replaced. Reality, not the model, is always the ultimate touchstone. Mathematical expression of the facts-in-relation leads to sharper analysis, rendering the knowledge based on the crude quantitative model more precise. But image-forming and model-making are the crucial steps in the whole process.

Many school hours should therefore be devoted to bringing out of the memory and into the imagination of the students some scene

91

or phenomenon known to the entire group, after which they should extract from the image details not known to be there on first observation. Unexpected recollection being an important resource for learning, it needs to be awakened in young persons, before the habit of recall-by-formula from an over organized and abstract memory blots out the full, rounded image imprinted by experience.

Recall from memory, it should be noted, is fallible, as witnesses in court frequently reveal. Recollection requires confirmation, but it remains a great stimulus to imaginative thinking and must be cultivated for that reason. To take an example: in one session, the exterior of the school building might be the subject of recall by the children—how tall is the door compared to one's own height? how many windows are there? An outline can be drawn on the board—a good preparation for graphing—then someone is sent outside to check on the accuracy of the group's conclusions. Exercises involving moving objects such as a man walking, a runner sprinting, and an automobile starting up and passing the runner can suggest the basic idea of positions changing with time, of varying velocities, and of acceleration.

Many other valuable ideas can be drawn out of the experience of young children: ideas of confirmation; of estimation; of less-than, greater-than, or equal-to, as well as making simple predictions which can be tested. The teacher's ingenuity will suggest a variety of topics and occasions to be seized. The spirit of the exercise is that of a game, everyone cooperating rather than competing. Collaboration is essential to scientific work and it should begin early.

The concept of measurement, with its arbitrary units, can be introduced as a supplement to estimation but not as replacement for it. Exploring of the foot as a unit of measure can be something of a recreational break: all the pupils are set to ascertaining the width of the room in multiples of their own feet, then, for purposes of communication, and agreement, deciding to use the familiar ruler ("one foot"') as the accepted unit.

The fact that scientific thinking arises in an interchange of information between people, necessitating an agreement on what different sorts of things are to be called and what they mean, enables young people to grasp the social nature of scientific formulation.

Basic then to the learning of science at this early stage are: first, the internal action of recalling an image as a preliminary to the formation of a model; and second, the external action of comparing the behavior the model leads one to expect with the actual behavior of objects when the conditions are changed. An early familiarity with these mental operations can reduce the difficulty that analytic and quantitative thinking often presents to the learner later, when science is introduced as a formal discipline.

In the first three years, didactic instruction in science should be minimal. A few "wonders" might be demonstrated, such as resonance in music, or a simple explanation of the angles of incidence and reflection, but only phenomena which are extremely simple should be considered. Complexity and the invoking of mysterious (purely verbal) explanations should be avoided during this critical period. If a field trip is made to a local planetarium, a model of the solar system might be introduced prudently and without looking down on the ideas of the ancients. Classification of plants or animals can be mentioned, but any reference to theory at this stage could easily be misleading.

Some biographical stories can be used to illustrate how the mind wonders and asks questions. Archimedes is a good possibility. A little closer to home, Benjamin Franklin provides several examples of the success of directed curiosity. It was he who named electricity arbitrarily as "positive" and "negative," the names still in use today. The common experience of rubbing one's feet on the carpet and getting a spark when one touches the doorknob can be used in relation to static electricity and linked with Franklin's experiment with the kite. Another story that can be told is that of energy—energy as food, energy as sunlight, energy stored, and energy expended. The idea that energy may take multiple forms, all of which can raise the temperature of a standard container of water, can be illustrated in simple ways.

In a word, science in the early grades should be an integral part of the story of the world that is being unfolded to the child, not separate from it or cited as authority. Scientific activity should be shown as a way of examining the universe, and the process might be described as follows: (1) an external object is observed and taken into the imagination in its wholeness; (2) pertinent characteristics are abstracted and named in the common language; (3) the object (or at least its image) is re-observed and confirmed; (4) a statement of meaning is presented to the community (the class).

The exercise in which the class imagines (or "images") the school building is handled in just this way, ending with a "graph" that "looks like" the building. The candle experiment can include the timing of a series of observations so that the imagination combines them and notes that twice as much air lets the candle burn twice as long. The fact that nothing "disappears" can be tested. The hypothesis that some component of the air is used up by the burning can be proposed and tested.

If the pupils engage in such mental operations, spontaneously offering explanations and proposing tests of their validity, the elementary teacher can be satisfied that science is being well taught.

SCIENCE IN THE MIDDLE YEARS

As the child advances, more sophisticated scientific statements can begin to be used. What was before a story with qualitative physical attributes can become a precise description of events with quantitative details. Although still not taught in separate courses by specialized teachers, science gradually emerges as a recognizable activity in the general subjects studied—geography, arithmetic, music, prosody—wherever the teacher finds pertinent opportunities to clarify or deepen understanding.

In these middle years from the fourth to the sixth grade, when progress is being made toward the study of science as a separate discipline, certain objectives can be set for skills and conceptual power. Estimation should become quantitative; distinctions should be made between different though related physical properties— for example, force, power, and energy; concepts of sequence and structure should by now be understandable.

Supposedly children become fully literate and numerically competent during these years; of almost equal importance to the development of their minds is the ability to represent experience in patterns—mapping and graphing. Maps are graphs of distance in one direction plotted against another, with time standing still. Street maps are good examples of this device. Countries and continents are similarly mapped from measurements of distances and directions at ground level. Only in recent years have we had visual confirmation of what had previously been mapped; satellite pictures show that coastlines which before were imaginary constructions fashioned out of surveyors' field notes really do have the shapes that were projected.

When time is one of the variables, the picture is not so direct. One might consider, for instance, the history of a school bus delivering its passengers after school. As a representation of the experience, one could plot the speed of the bus against time with its various stoppings and startings and its traveling at different rates. The speedometer and odometer of the automobile can be used to advantage here. From these exercises motion as a quan-

95

titative concept is established. Thus a graph is made showing how far the bus has travelled as a function of time, a visual representation of experience. Later, when the calculus is introduced, these same graphs can be reconsidered with a more powerful analysis.

The life of the child is rich in experiences that can be interpreted by the method of science. A seesaw, for instance, can introduce the beam balance for the comparison of masses, an informal experiment being fashioned by putting a weight at each end of the ruler, and the class being asked to find the balance point between them. Once more the concept of arbitrary units occurs, this time the unit of mass.

Static electricity, already mentioned, can provide an impromptu experiment on a dry day, leading to the discovery of two kinds of electricity, with like charges repelling, unlike attracting. Every interpretation and addition to the number of well-defined terms arouses a desire for more understanding of the world around us. At the same time, these experiments provide opportunities for the introduction of algebraic equations. A separate chapter in this book is devoted to mathematics, but the teacher of science knows that mathematics is inseparable from experimentation and must be taught while teaching the natural sciences.

The romance and excitement evoked by learning to deal with the universe in *quantitative* terms, rather than by means of qualitative verbal description should be frequently emphasized. One of the great intellectual accomplishments of a civilized person is the ability to compare two quantities to a precision of four or five significant figures. It sets such a person apart from every other living organism. Not only does it make possible remarkable practical achievements, but it also imparts the gratifying quality of elegance to the patterns through which existence is perceived.

In the seventh and eighth grades, whether instruction is departmentalized and under the direction of specialists or remains in the hands of a general teacher, science instruction becomes systematic. Experiment becomes part of everything learned in the subject. Indeed, in the seventh year, experiments, repeated, discussed, and repeated again, should constitute the main part of the course. A very small number of experiments should be performed during one school year, perhaps one each in physics, chemistry, and biology—and no more than two hours each week should be spent in the process. What is being introduced is a way of thinking, not a quantity of information. The individual event needs to be explored, more and more deeply in each successive session.

Each experiment should have a particular purpose—to answer a question, to discover the law underlying an observed phenomenon, to determine the value of a physical constant, and so on. Experimentation should never be a mere playing around to see what happens. In experimentation, that is, laboratory work, coaching is essential. Experiment involves the handling of instruments and materials. Not only accuracy, but safety frequently depends upon careful procedures. But coaching must go beyond simple practical guidance in how things are done. In the laboratory, coaching must inquire into why they are done. Every step has a reason for being included and each reason must become clear to the students taking part in the experiment.

In discussing each experiment after it is done, criticisms must be elicited—what of the planning, the execution, the analysis of the data, and the interpretation? The teacher's function here is group tutoring in the art of pointed criticism. At the end, the students discuss in Socratic fashion what kind of knowledge has been gained, the teacher leading them to examine more deeply the implications of their work. There are unsolved problems close to the particular operations carried out, as well as more remote and abstract issues, that may reach as far as the limits of man's scientific knowledge. All these matters deserve discussion.

Meanwhile, all students are to write papers describing their individual work, using where available their own data, and reaching their own conclusions. Students must be trained to write the results of experiments in simple and precise fashion. Only in this way can the teacher be sure that important insight into the experimental results has been achieved. The ability to translate observations, impressions, and insights into precise and concise sentences is an absolute requirement in a program of science for all.

The first experiments are purely empirical, coming as they do before any theory is known, even before mathematical preparation is adequate for quantitative theory. For each experiment the teacher is prepared to explain the problem and the objective sought. He is ready to promise that before the students finish high school they will have developed theory and quantitative methods adequate to explain the phenomenon they have observed. For the present, results remain in the realm of discovered empirical law.

## THE PENDULUM EXPERIMENT

Since at this level, too, the first experiments should be simple, consider the operation of a pendulum. One might begin by reading pertinent passages from Galileo's *Two New Sciences*, beginning (say) on page 95 of the Dover edition. Some three paragraphs along, the statement is made: ". . . as to the times of vibration of bodies suspended by threads, . . . . the squares of the times are proportional to the lengths of the thread." Written as an equation, this statement is:

$$T^2 = k \cdot l$$

where $T$ is the "period" of the pendulum (the time for one complete swing back and forth), $l$ is its length, and $k$ stands for the constant proportion between time and length that Galileo supposes true.

Here, obviously, is a statement that can be checked by experiment. The assignment is to perform the experiment superficially, with students working in pairs, determining the period of the pendulum (a plum bob on the end of a string will do nicely) by timing many swings and measuring the length of the string, repeating the operation for several different lengths, then graphing the "period squared" against the length.

[Example: the length from the point of suspension to the middle of the bob is measured as 4 ft. The time for ten swings is 22 seconds. The period $T$ then is 2.2 sec. and the period squared is 4.84 sec$^2$. On ordinary graph paper a small cross is placed 4 units (ft.) to the left of zero and 4.8 units (sec$^2$) up from zero. The notation is repeated for several lengths. If the points on the paper when joined together form a nearly straight line, then the group realizes that there may be something to the hypothesis and that it is worth careful study.]

The next time, the experiment is repeated carefully with several determinations at each length and the possible range of error noted for each value of length. The best value of the constant $k$ is determined from the data, and its range of variation recorded. (In the example above, $k = 1.21$ sec$^2$/ft.)

Now a critique is made of the experiment. Are the variations in the value of $k$ within what one would expect from the possibilities for error in the method? Are there any systematic errors, such as might occur in measuring the period if the count begins with one instead of zero? Is the center of mass properly determined? To settle these questions it may be necessary to do the experiment again.

When each pair of pupils has determined the best value for $k$, the class averages its results and states the range of the observed deviations. Then the teacher reveals that, according to theory, the value of $k$ is 2 $pi$ squared divided by $g$, where $g$ is the acceleration due to gravity. A little didactic instruction ensues and the value of $g$ is calculated, including the units of length and time used in the measurements.

Comparison can be made with the known local value for $g$, but an attempt at agreement is not the purpose of the experiment: the purpose is the confirmation of Galileo's conjecture. Not only is a knowledge of scientific fact gained but an awareness of the human traits involved in trial-and-error as well.

Reading on in Galileo, we find he makes a further claim: the period is absolutely unaffected by the angle through which the pendulum swings. The truth of this statement can be checked by experiment, for large and small angles. Deviations from the law can be looked for and, if found, they must be explained.

In an extended experiment such as has been described, the teacher faces the difficulty of avoiding tedium. Many students are likely to tire of the game unless the problem before them is continually restated. Student pressure tends to induce the teacher to supply "cookbook" formulas so that laboratory work can be performed and then dismissed, the cooks never tasting the broth they are concocting. But in learning science, experiment is meant primarily to open up and keep opening the imagination, as begun in the early grades. In making use of incremental repetition, experimentation teaches care and accuracy in observation and measurement, of course, but its real purpose is to make clear the fact of a relation between mind and the external world, thus establishing an attitude needed for all further scientific understanding.

An equivalent experiment in chemistry and one in biology complete the study of science in the seventh grade. These experiments require little theory but must adequately represent the basic methods of the disciplines. The next year, a course that cuts across the disciplines can be presented—earth science, for instance—still making relatively little use of theory and pointing to the ways of obtaining information. A second possibility is a course in astronomy. These courses serve to orient the student in the larger physical world.

## DISCUSSIONS AND SEMINARS DURING THE MIDDLE YEARS

The Socratic method of asking questions is an ideal way to make the pupil grasp the difference between an opinion and a deduction. A simple problem in probability might illustrate the point. The old story of three pairs of white socks and three of black in a drawer will serve; or, in the classroom, six red marbles and six blue ones in a box. The question is: if blindfolded, how many marbles (or socks) would one have to take out to be certain of getting a pair?

The question of the probability of getting a pair of a given color on the first two draws is more complicated but well within the capabilities of a fourth grader. Then the class can investigate three draws, four draws, and so on. A table of probabilities can be written on the blackboard. Then an experiment can be conducted, each child determining how many draws are required to obtain a pair, repeating the process several times and comparing the actual results with the calculated probabilities. The comparison is not likely to be exact. Deductions do not necessarily lead to certainty. Probabilistic predictions grow more certain with an increasing number of trials. For experimental science, and, indeed, for most of life's situations, probabilistic mathematics is at least as important as exact relationships.

The discussion of experimental method—something more than a demonstration—is an excellent device for an introduction to "real" science. For instance, once the child understands area and volume, the maximum length of a molecule of oil can be determined by a method Benjamin Franklin introduced. A drop of oil whose volume is carefully measured in an eye-dropper is placed on water in a pan large enough for the spreading oil slick not to touch the edges. The area of the slick is determined as accurately as possible. The volume divided by the area is then the thickness of the oil slick and is the length of the molecule, assuming that the oil forms a single-molecule layer, as it is likely to do.

A seminar is the place for discussions based on assigned readings, some of which will concern science. The readings assigned should be clear, understandable, and reasonably short. Recommended works are listed in the Appendix, from which, most often, only short sections can be assigned. These readings are not intended to teach science directly but to raise issues for discussion. For example, Galileo's *Dialogue Concerning the Two Chief World Systems* can lead to questions about what we actually know and what we think we know.

It would be well for the teacher of these middle years to develop interest in and knowledge of the history of science. *The Edge of Objectivity,* by C. C. Gillespie, might be a good place to start, and Thomas Kuhn's modern classic *The Structure of Scientific Revolutions* is strongly advised for anyone who would teach science. Libraries contain many other good books on this subject. The heroes of science are many; their stories are highly instructive. The great *Dictionary of Scientific Biography* is an invaluable source of information, not only about the lives of the scientists, but also about the conditions, difficulties, and contributions associated with their work.

## SCIENCE IN THE UPPER YEARS

In the last four years of schooling in science, theory is dominant. Instruction should be mainly didactic, the lectures interlaced with questioning and *ad hoc* illustrations. Still, problem-solving and laboratory experiment are performances by students that will require coaching. These are time-consuming activities for the teacher, but they are essential to efficient learning, as well as evidence that learning has, indeed, occurred.

Even so, at this stage learning is by no means a process of storing information or mastering methods. Everything that enters the memory must be interpreted and made to fit into a structure of understanding, which is in effect the scientific mode of knowing. Thus nuggets of information acquired by the student are instances, illustrations, sometimes paradigms that furnish the structure and extend its use.

Young persons who have been through a Paideia Program in the lower grades, even if they are of widely varying abilities, should be adequately prepared for secondary study of greater exactitude but without substituting exactitude for understanding. The courses must be designed for general students, not those with a particular scientific bent, although the material must be such as to engage also the best minds. Consequently, the teacher must be well prepared, enthusiastic about the subject, and sympathetic to the varying needs of students. The teachers of science should meet frequently, forming their own "academy of science," and helping each other to design the common curriculum. They must themselves continue to be learners.

Of the three major sciences, physics is the most basic, biology the most complex, and chemistry something of a bridge between them. Each has its own mode of thought, but in recent years they have been drawn together and now strongly interpenetrate each other. The initial course, in the ninth grade, can take advantage of this interpenetration by presenting materials drawn from the three sciences. The central theme might be energy, the principal subject the structure of matter, and the extension of these things into the systems of biology.

The course would begin with electricity, central to all three disciplines, and though mechanics could be resorted to for definitions of such quantities as force and energy, both kinetic and potential, the electron-volt becomes the usual unit of energy employed. The atom would be introduced with the Bohr model, but the picture should quickly shift to energy levels associated with the four quantum numbers, giving rise to the periodic table.

Chemistry would take over at atomic and molecular levels. The nature of the forces between atoms will lead to the use of the periodic table to explain how chemical properties change with the increasing atomic weight of the elements. The concept of valence and the three-dimensional structures of atoms and molecules can be conveyed by means of the same kinds of presentations described in the discussions dealing with physics.

What is suggested by such a course is not a beginning with simple things and moving to more complex ones. Rather, moderately advanced theories are chosen to represent the disciplines in a more or less connected fashion, each accurately presented, but not fully developed from the most basic principles. Such a treatment provides firm reference points within each science, together with obvious interconnections, so that the courses that follow are never wholly separate or irrelevant. Laboratory projects should be designed to familiarize students with instruments and measuring techniques. The principles of null reading devices, such as bridges and potentiometers, should be stressed. This first year of upper-level work should emphasize carefulness, precision, and ingenuity. Its role is to prepare for the following three years. The course syllabus, including laboratory work and seminars, should be developed by the science staff in awareness of the concurrent advance in the students' mathematical knowledge.

In the three succeeding years, courses in chemistry, biology, and physics should be offered, in that order. Physics, the most mathematical of the sciences, is placed last in order to correlate with the most advanced mathematics. The teachers should be aware of the stress that these two severe courses place on the students in their senior year and be prepared to temper the wind.

The level of the courses should be about that of the present introductory college courses, but the number of topics would need to be considerably reduced. The principle of thorough coverage of a few topics is to be followed—not for thoroughness' sake, but for depth of understanding. It is likely that new textbooks would need to be prepared.

The chemistry and biology courses might be considered, perhaps even renamed, a two-year course in molecular studies. The biological universe with its unbelievably variegated living forms, the amazing beauty of the patterns into which they have evolved, and the almost unbelievable powers of sensing and reacting to their environment which they possess form a picture without which the human imagination is greatly impoverished. The demonstration that all living things on earth exhibit a common central molecular pattern of life processes involving DNA, RNA and proteins makes it difficult to believe that life has had more than one successful origin. The power and elegance of the genetic process and the molecular basis of biological reproduction and the regulation of cellular activities cannot but impress all students and help them to develop reverence for all life, but especially for human life.

It is imperative to point out how man is an animal sharing with every kind of living organism a wide variety of basic structures and processes. At the same time, it is equally important to demonstrate how man is unique and that no other living form even approaches the sensitivities and capacities of the human mind or the complexities of human needs.

It is impossible to imagine young people at whatever age who will not be spellbound to hear about the DNA revolution and the present status of our understanding of human biology, ranging from its molecular and cellular structure to the fantastic story of the current conception of the human developmental process. The various functions of our bodies, ranging from the power to manufacture antibodies which protect us from invaders, to the role of brain hormones and biochemical processes that affect our unique ability to think, feel, communicate, store memories and manipulate abstractions, reveal the enormous potentialities contained within our bodies. The new powers of biological science and the realization of the new opportunities to solve many of the great enigmas of human biology can become the focus of a presentation that will inspire young people to feel renewed hope and dedication to the finding of new solutions to many of mankind's problems.

The senior-year physics course is easier to conceive. In outline it is simple: mechanics (as the basis of theory), electromagnetism including optics, quantum physics and the solid state; elementary particles and the consequences of indeterminacy. But the actual design must reflect the constraints of time and stress mentioned above.

At the beginning it may be advantageous to spend some class time in simply reading the text. When faced with a sudden jump in the level of reading, with new sets of references and new images to be formed, many students balk, supposing their minds are of the sort that cannot think in the fashion demanded. They need to be helped over the barrier by persistent coaching. They need to hear the words spoken, to have ideas ordered at the pace of speech, not of sight. More than explication of ideas, it is the sense of a total form that must be communicated. Even good students enjoy having their understanding confirmed by hearing the words spoken.

This sort of exercise, done informally with individual students and from time to time with the entire class, promotes cohesion in a group made up of varying abilities. The kind of equality that the Paideia Program sponsors is not one of averaging, never a diminishment of the best, but rather a patient leading of all toward the best, by varying pedagogical methods.

The assumption of equality rests on a recognition that intellect is part of the humanity everyone shares, that thought is a common ground open to all, and that, though some minds travel faster and farther, all communicate on the same plane.

SEMINARS IN THE UPPER YEARS

Seminars run on Socratic lines reach their full importance during these upper years of secondary school. Documents for discussion chosen from the history of science serve to inculcate a respect, even a piety, for the past and allow students to participate in the creative process of discovery. The seminars themselves will frequently center on questions pertinent to present society but rooted in cultures of the past. Each of the scientific disciplines has its classics. Several have been listed in the Appendix. A little research on the part of the teacher will reveal unexpected riches of thought.

CONCLUSION

An understanding of science is exceedingly important in achieving the ends of education for the young; it prepares for

(1) earning a living, (2) being a good citizen, (3) leading a full life enriched by continued learning. The increasing dependence of the economy on science makes evident this importance for the first goal, and the cultural significance of science similarly serves the third. A few words more may be said about the second goal.

Democracies have a special need for universal schooling in science, because critical decisions involving the health and security of the people as a nation—decisions that are pervasively scientific and technological—must be made by the general public, by the electorate. Not only specialists but all people must be competent to make these decisions, either through direct knowledge or through sufficient understanding to recognize the authentic from the false in those who advise them. The outcome is crucial to democracy.

Furthermore, a lack of understanding of science has divided the common consciousness. A proper schooling in science can re-align the planes of thought, reconcile attitudes, and help restore and maintain the essential equality to which a democratic regime is committed.

D.C. & T.P.

# 7
## History

HISTORY, as its name indicates, is first of all a story. It tells what happened at a certain time and place to certain persons and peoples. Or to put it more generally, history as a school subject is the account of human actions in the past. Because it is a story, some part of history can be taught to small children, and it is recommended here that such stories become part of the curriculum toward the end of kindergarten and be continued in the first grade for the six-year-olds.

The idea of "once upon a time" and "many years ago" gives a good first grasp upon history if it is attached to some interesting incidents and episodes and linked with good pictures or slides. For example: Benjamin Franklin drawing down the lightning through his kite; the Pony Express before trains and planes; Columbus' trouble with his sailors and his vindication by the discovery of land—the list of possibilities is virtually endless. The aim is to show that many curious events took place before the child was born and that there are ways of learning about them. What should be left in the young mind is: the doings and the names of men and women who actually lived on this earth "like you and me" and the vision of their dress, hairstyles, equipment, and modes of speech.

With these fundamentals should go the notion that each of us has a history of our own, each of us is part of the stream of history. Some portion of our share in events is known to our family and friends, some of it stays inside us, in memory, where our reasons for doing things and our purpose in doing them will probably remain hidden. Yet "one of us in this class" may in the future be "important historically." How then will later comers know his or her history? How do we know what Franklin, Columbus, and the rest thought and did? They told us, directly or indirectly. While they lived or soon after, journalists, historians, and biographers put together what was said and done, by the actors and by the witnesses, and this is how we come to have histories and "lives" (biographies) of the great. From all these—the "contemporary record"—the stories so far learned in this class have been chosen.

It should be added that a well-read and imaginative teacher is often able to do more than I have suggested here. For example, men and women now living who are products of public schools remember hearing and reading at the age of eight or nine about the American Indians. Two or three weeks were devoted to the subject, which opened the young minds to a number of important things: if, as is believable, the Indians came from Asia, what is Asia? It is a continent, far away on the other side of the Pacific ocean. The Indians over here were not all alike; they belonged to many tribes with different customs. Some were allied with the English colonists (what are "colonists"?); others were hostile and allied with the French (where is France?). Indian ways of getting their living varied from region to region; Indians differed in the works of art they produced and the beliefs they held about divinity. Taken all together, there was a *pre-Columbian* culture—remember Columbus? and the date of his arrival?—where? All this is part of American history, which you are sure to study later.

Beyond this point, the teaching of history in school should proceed cautiously; for as a fully developed subject, history involves

110

adult motives and complex institutions that young children can take but little interest in—for example, the fight over a National Bank, state sovereignty, the franchise, or press censorship. It is therefore recommended that the study of history in continuous fashion should not begin until the seventh grade. Between the first and the seventh grades, the importance of history and interest in it should be sustained simply by reading and discussing more and more complex stories of the past. Teachers of English who assign stories to read, and teachers of science as they come to great principles, should be asked to make historical points about authors and discoverers and should say something about their lives and works, reinforcing the idea that the consequences of history are with us still, present all the time; we not only make history but are bathed in it.

By the age of 13 or 14, the adult concerns that make up the staple of written history have begun to arouse the interest of youth. At home or at school, in print or on television, they have heard of elections, wars, strikes, treaties, diplomacy, and other features of public life. It is the time to draw on these casual noises from the big world and unite them into an increasingly coherent recital of their meaning, which is to say their origins and purposes. The study of these matters should properly begin with American history.

Why American history? Because it requires the least amount of explanation about the details of culture and society. Most of these are familiar, close at hand, understood without effort—as the corresponding details of ancient Egypt or modern China are not.

But at this point, the scheme of instruction must change altogether from what it has been for the lower grades. It must no longer rely for interest on anecdotes, vignettes of the past, and quaint features of olden times—bits and pieces. The essence of genuine history is *continuity* and its main characteristic is *combination* (often *confusion*) of acts, hopes, plans, moves, efforts, failures, triumphs, tragedies—all these arising from the behavior of persons living at a certain time and place.

It follows that "a history course" must cover as many aspects of a period as possible, a period being a sizable span of time—a century at the very least. Near the present day or distant from it, the means of arousing and sustaining interest are always there, because points of comparison are never lacking. For example, if the course begins with the Civil War, the 20th century struggle for civil rights is there to provide a link with the issues of the past. If the starting point is 1776 and the War of Independence, modern anti-colonialism and wars for nationhood supply parallels. If it is the landing of the Pilgrims, it is clear that the story of freedom of thought and social betterment is far from over and done with.

But parallels must be wisely spaced and not overdrawn. The aim is to show similarity within difference; otherwise the point of history—the pastness of the past—is lost. The valuable lesson to keep in mind is that emotional and intellectual sympathy with other ways than ours can be achieved and enjoyed.

These aims and efforts in a 7th-grade course should result in the student's permanent possession of a sense of time—the Pilgrims did not arrive in grandma's time, but much earlier, several grandmas back. After many similar perceptions the centuries begin to acquire their proper look; the student has been endowed with a sense of history. Here is the opportunity to show the value and importance of dates. They are not just a cruel strain on the memory for the sake of passing exams; they are pegs on which to hang clusters of events that share a common time and a related significance. If presented and explained as markings—buoys or lighthouses on the ocean of history—dates will be remembered and used with very little effort.

The 7th-grade course should leave in the mind a sense of rationality about the past. What is called the "logic of events" must begin to be felt. Logic and rationality do not mean reasonableness. Human acts often spring from mad, wild, impulses; but the later observer can rationally see how ambition, revenge, greed, ignorance, hope, habit, idealism, practicality and unpracticality interact to produce the results that we know occurred. That is what is meant by the logic of events. It is part of the historical sense, a way of understanding that has a most useful result: it makes any part of history a recognizably human affair, something that shows what human beings really did and thought. The student who reads history will unconsciously develop what is the highest value of history: judgment in worldly affairs. This is a permanent good, not because "history repeats"—we can never exactly match past and present situations—but because the "tendency of things" shows an amazing uniformity within any given civilization. As the great historian Burckhardt said of historical knowledge, it is not "to make us more clever the next time, but wiser for all time."

The object of the course should be learning the full story *as* history, that is to say as facts and meanings the pupil can recite and write about in well-organized consecutive portions with a sense of their continuity. The 7th- or 8th-grade course should form a strong "priming coat" over which later courses can paint in greater detail the unfolding of the American story and its main characters. The same principle will hold true of any offerings in ancient history, European history, or English history.

This simple well-defined purpose cannot be achieved by using the familiar gimmicks and pretentious "methods." Beyond the elementary grades, where charades are harmless, there should be no play-acting, literal or metaphorical. Impersonating William Penn and the Indians once again may be fun, but it is a waste of valuable time, it distracts from true study, and it gives disproportionate emphasis to episodes as against large events and movements.

113

It is no less play-acting to go through the motions of "research." The word should not even occur, for at that level the thing is non-existent. A report on reading is a fine exercise and it should be called just that, which is its proper name. Even average students see through make-believe; they know they are only fooling around when "Egyptian religion" is first "researched," then "acted out" by the whole class.

Teachers brought up on "methods" may be convinced that good teaching consists in a succession of such "imaginative" devices, to make history "come alive" and keep the class "excited" about learning. But observation and interviews with the young suggest, on the contrary, that these exercises induce boredom in those who want to learn and are taken as relief from work by those who do not. Excitement, anyway, is an occasional feeling and not the proper mood for learning. One begins to wonder whether it is not the teacher who likes discontinuity and interruption as a substitute for serious work.

In social studies, the field trip has its proper place, but its counterpart in a history course, which is the visit to some local site or museum, has not much value. The monument or battleground or Indian relic is apt to lack important connection with anything learned and thus remain just another episode. The "come alive" idea is, incidentally, a foolish cliché. A good teacher will so present, relate, and discuss with the class the facts to be learned that he or she will steadily stir up the imaginations of the listening class. History is not dead and does not need resuscitation; it lives in our habits of thought and our institutions, our prejudices and our purposes, and what the history course does is to tell how these things and thoughts came to be as they are.

But what, aside from discussing—turning over and forming opinions—shall the young students do? Read, first and last. History is for reading and developing a taste for reading history ensures lifelong pleasure. Let some striking portion of Prescott's *Conquest of Mexico* be assigned to a few students, to be read and turned into a *precis,* the best among them to be read aloud in class. Other small groups can read and write something on the same subject, or a similar one. Teach the students to be good critics of what they read—which means, to know how to praise as well as criticize it, but not to moralize.

To find origins and trace the story down to ourselves, as suggested, one may go back a short distance—say, two hundred years—or a much longer one, like two thousand. In either case, one must be sure that the line of descent is clear and genuine. This prime requirement brings up the question frequently debated—what to do about world history? To learn about the United States only, or even about Western civilization, is not enough. We live in "one world" and children today should be taught about Asiatic cultures and African. The countries of that large tract of earth—runs the argument—are going to affect our lives in future, have already done so. They can boast old and admirable civilizations too, and if we are to get along with their modern descendants we must learn to appreciate their heritage. To neglect doing so is to show ourselves narrow and provincial, ignorant of the greater and more populous part of the world.

This reasoning sounds plausible and enlightened, but it deals in abstractions and it loses its force once these are reduced to concrete particulars. To begin with, the study of any people's history requires a familiarity with innumerable facts, customs, and institutions that do not get into the textbooks. The pupil knows about his own people from simply living where he does. He or she understands what houses look like, what being married means, and why people go to church or to an election booth. The very words for these and a thousand other things, as well as the motives and feelings linked with the actions or conditions they de-

115

note, do not need to be taught at all: they are the well-known facts of daily life. But as soon as one starts reading about another civilization, the corresponding facts all differ. They are obscure or mistaken until one has painfully learned a set of other customs, institutions, purposes and emotions—a strange world that cannot be quickly grasped. The terms themselves, even when they look like ours, are charged with different connotations—for example, "family feeling" here and in China, where ancestor worship has been omnipotent.

There are other obstacles, too. For example, the terms Asiatic and African do not mean simply two or more nations. Each covers wide territories and diversified peoples and cultures, forming an indefinitely large number of "subjects." Each—or some—of these may be a proper study for social science, but we can hardly claim to know their *history*. To suppose they *have* only *one* history is the first mistake, as when we lump together "Oriental" things. What is meant by "Oriental"? Is it Chinese, and if so, Northern or Southern or Mandarin? Is it Japanese or Korean? Is it Javanese or Cambodian? Is it Indian (Hindu) or Pakistani (Moslem)? Is it Tibetan or Sri-Lankian—? One could go on asking and each new name would point to a notably different culture. In short, what we face is several lifetimes of work to master diverse histories, each remote from that of New England or Texas, between which we ourselves see enough differences to require special effort in the teaching of a unified American history.

What may we conclude? Are American school children to remain "provincial" in the sense of knowing only the history of the West? Two answers suggest themselves. First, "world history" is a term that can apply to information that varies in depth—deeper "at home" (wherever home may be) than elsewhere. It is still a kind of knowledge of the world to know *that* something exists or took place, and even something of what it amounted to, without presuming to say how it was and is regarded by those in whose country it occurred. Every educated mind shows this variation in depth and range: natural limitations make encyclopedic knowledge an impossibility.

But there is nonetheless great value in knowing the *that* and—to a small extent—the *what*. It so happens—to come back to the difficulties of world history—that a good course in modern European history necessarily brings in the existence, and makes clear the importance, of the rest of the world. It brings in the western hemisphere with Columbus and cannot thereafter cut loose from it—European and American history are intertwined.

So are European history and the histories of Africa and Asia. For good and evil, colonialism knitted together the destinies of all the peoples of the earth. In that part of the European story, the student learns—superficially but existentially—all that he can absorb of non-Western history, short of mastering the languages and the stories of the peoples involved.

If such a student has a good grounding in history, a sense of history and a taste for reading it, his first, superficial awareness of those other great civilizations will—if he wishes—enable him to deepen that knowledge, by himself, and thus extend his human sympathies and worldly judgment in the unique way that the study of history makes possible.

## HOW TO PROCEED: SOME FURTHER DETAILS

Any knowledge of history, however elementary, must be linked from the start with an awareness of where the persons talked of lived, where the events took place. That awareness means: geography. It is best to start talking of geography by referring to places known, at least by name, in the neighborhood—the river, the hill, the mountain ridge seen in the distance, the flats on the other

117

side of the stream. Then perhaps the outline map that is given out does not give false impression of wide open spaces, all white and convenient for settlements and battles to occur in. Ideally, the bare outline to be colored and filled in with names should always be coupled with a physical map showing mountains, forests, and other features. In class, attention should be paid to soil, climate, rainfall, and the other drawbacks or advantages that the earth affords to making a livelihood and developing a civilization: "Why are large cities so often on large rivers? Why did it take so long to settle our continent all the way to California?"

Together with the sense of place, the learner of history must develop a sense of time. This is not easy to do—*or to teach*. How does one get to feel a difference between 100 years ago, 500 and 1500? Well, 100 years ago may be "when grandfather's father was alive," or "when the city hall was built—you can see the date on the cornerstone." So far, so good. But to stretch that feeling by merely saying or thinking some multiple of 100 such as five or fifteen is not likely to yield results. There must be objects to associate with a time considerably remote. For example, a portrait of Queen Elizabeth I, the Holbein painting of Henry VIII, a drawing of a ship of the Tudor navy; George and Martha Washington in their costumes; the facade of Mount Vernon; the streets of Philadelphia. Conditions, states of mind, can help when made vivid: when Benjamin Franklin drew down the lightning, what exactly was known about electricity? And why should Sir Walter Raleigh lay down his cloak (what's a cloak?) for the queen to cross a mud patch? How were cities built, kept clean, and policed?

The specific offering of courses must be left to the best judgment of the teacher or department, in keeping with the part of the country or the school population to be served. As an indication of a desirable sequence, the following subjects may be listed as furnishing a conspectus of the historical bases of Western civilization: American History (seventh grade); History of England (eighth); Europe Since 1500 (ninth); Ancient Greece and Rome (tenth); The Middle Ages (eleventh); American History Since 1865 (twelfth).

As to the kinds of teaching recommended for the Paideia curriculum: coaching, lecturing, and discussing are all required, but they require a word or two concerning their application to the study of history. *Coaching* means giving out reading assignments, with suitable warnings about special difficulties, main points to look for, and the like. The reading is to be followed by recitation in class. But recitation must never be literal or by rote. In one 12th year class where the teacher asked "Who was Petrarch?" one student answered "He was the vanguard of the new emphasis." Those words from the textbook, but out of context, mean just nothing; learning done in that way amounts to zero. The able teacher, even in recitation time, manages to throw in elements of discussion, especially when an answer is off the point, incomplete, or unlikely: "Do you really think President Washington could have *ordered* all those foreign agents out of the country? Is that something that can be done—at any time?" The teacher will remember, and remind the students that history shows "how things go."

The drill connected with coaching is done through map work, looking up facts and visual materials, and short quizzes in which names and dates are "identified" in one short sentence. A ten-minute quiz, once a week, covering in part the previous week's work and including one or two items from earlier, can be made into a challenge. It is for *training*, not for displaying individual ability and passing the course.

In *lecturing* (which should be brief in span and subject matter), dates must be used as indicated earlier: they are pegs for hanging numbers of events and individual actions. With their aid, vivid mental associations are formed and built into solid knowledge as the number and variety of items accumulates in the memory with less and less effort: history is what you like to remember. Nor is the simple organizing of dates all that matters; there is the thought "two years before 1789" or "only one year after 1812," or "meanwhile in England during the same month." In short, relations, connections, contrasts, oddities, form the substance of what is talked about in the lecture give-and-take and the talk itself shows how one "historical mind" works with its materials.

Last comes the Socratic consecutive *discussion* of historical events and personalities. "What is there to discuss?—it all took place precisely thus and so, as the book says." Not true: different books give different accounts of the same event and period; estimates of the men and women involved present contrasting or contradictory portraits. It follows that for an informed discussion the students must be given readings from various authors. Some of the readings should show an historian taking up evidence that points in different directions and discussing it, sifting the pros and cons to reach a conclusion "on the balance of the evidence."

Seeing how this is done, and also how equally honest minds arrive at opposite views, is one of the eye-opening results of reading history. In the course of comparing, judging, doubting, and concluding for themselves, the students discover the actual spectacle of human affairs, relive its confusion, and learn that it continues to be as complex. No one is the infallible witness of his own time or the perfectly fair judge of character and action. A pluralism of views is unavoidable. With distance from the issues, a truer perspective can be had; one may be more equitable in judgment; but there are always not two sides but many sides to every question.

Thus reading about the debate on the adoption of the U.S. Constitution or the struggles of the Protestant Reformation affords a vicarious experience which is formative, quite apart from what the memory may retain of the facts. And when the mind has grasped in several contexts the effect of circumstance, the nature of partisanship, the role of chance, and the influence of leaders and bunglers, the student of history who has discussed with others these potent imponderables may become not only a better judge of public policy and politicians, but also a more tolerant person.

The teacher who conducts a discussion on readings in history should start out with a definite historical question, and it should never be, who was right or wrong, but what was possible at such and such a juncture? What could so-and-so have done, or refrained from doing, to achieve *this* purpose? Was the purpose really in the interests of the group he or she was leading? Were other choices open?—and so on. Every student's spoken contribution to the discussion should meet the point made just before, to amplify, correct, or refute it. Errors of fact must naturally be caught up, by questioning inaccurate statements and having another student supply the truth; for no argument can rest on a false basis. All assertions other than factual reminders must be accompanied by reasons: What is the evidence for what you say? What reasoning leads you to conclude as you do? The whole group may possibly settle some issue with unanimity, but more often diversity will prevail, one or more groups and individuals being persuaded or confirmed each in a different position. And that too is highly instructive.

J.B.

# 8
## Social Studies*

SOCIAL STUDIES IN THE CONTEXT OF
HISTORY AND GEOGRAPHY

THE STUDY of history outlined in the previous chapter is central to understanding the world in which we live. But it is not enough. It must be pursued in conjunction with a study of the peoples of the world, their relationship to their environment and to the institutions that structure their lives.

Many of these subjects are currently covered in social studies courses that tend to be superficial and are often considered marginal to the curriculum. The studies we propose are, on the contrary, an essential part of the preparation of students for our society, in which every citizen must have a basic understanding of how that society works, of how our nation relates to the other nations of the world, and of the ways in which human beings affect the world in which they live. To this end, teachers of social stud-

---

*Unlike other chapters in Part Two of this book, which attempt to select from their disciplines what can be accomplished in the twelve years of basic schooling, this chapter spreads before the reader an extremely wide range of topics, problems, issues, and materials that belong to social studies.

It is assumed that teachers will choose from this rich offering what they deem feasible and best to cover in the time available. They are certainly not expected to deal with all matters here suggested as appropriate to the role played by social studies in the curriculum. M.J.A.

ies will have to make connections between subject matter proper to the natural sciences, the social sciences, and the humanities. They should not expect, however, nor should they be asked, to convey the substance of self-contained disciplines, such as anthropology, economics, political science, psychology, and sociology, which have their own conceptual frameworks. The study of these belongs at the post-secondary level of schooling, after a basic acquaintance with social studies has been achieved.

Social studies are not to be understood as independent of history, or as a substitute for it. The historical approach affords perspective, the chance to compare ourselves and our institutions with others in the past. This is necessary if students are to develop the habit of thinking critically, of asking for relevant evidence and information, of looking behind appearances and beneath words to reality. History's creative power comes from its narrative character, its ordering of reality, its revelation of consequence and development. It is the indispensable grounding for the social sciences and social studies, which are otherwise prone to abstraction, thematic treatment, and random case studies.

Nor is geography to be forgotten. As history directs us to the actual experiences of people through time, geography gives us the settings of human endeavor all over the planet. In its concern with the relatedness of nature and human kind, geography—physical as well as human—offers students an understanding of the world of work built upon hard fact. The need to work begins with the environment itself—what is there, what is not there, what must be constructed or grown or produced, what must somehow be acquired or done without.

Learning about these matters can begin in the earliest grades. Young students who examine the growth of the continents, the formations of the mountains and the seas, and the formation and location of the natural resources as matters of natural science will

123

also come to understand how each of these occurrences affects humankind, how weather patterns and systems have altered the surface of the earth over time, and how such patterns influence people and the ways in which they live. Likewise, the study of natural resources and their distribution, and of soils and vegetation, including crops and crop production, provides a basis for exploring the relationships of all of these to the earth's population, the use and the abuse of resources, and the development of economic systems.

Eventually students will learn that people in every part of the world are concerned with the same basic problems: finding food and shelter, procuring jobs and health care, devising systems of justice and government, defining and protecting property, and explaining natural phenomena that at first seem impossible to understand. Such an appreciation of the universal human condition—common needs, common struggles to fill them—is the first, essential step toward respect for peoples and cultures foreign to our own. And, once students learn that there are many ways— some better, some worse—of solving human problems, and many different notions of life, work, or culture even in their own society, they will be responsive to the idea that human existence, while showing certain of the same characteristics everywhere, is nevertheless too various in its forms to judge without broad study and careful consideration.

SOCIAL STUDIES AND CIVIC HABITS

Telling people how to be good citizens is not the same as preparing them for the task. Citizens ultimately learn through practice: they become active and wise participants in the community when they have the opportunity to bring their knowledge, skills, and abilities to bear on a given issue. But social studies provide an understanding of the institutions and proceedings that are involved.

Students must learn how their government works, how decisions are made, and how they can influence those decisions. They need to understand something of the fundamental principles that shaped our nation and, through discussion, to consider how well they have been applied. Knowledge of the conflicts—of war and peace, wealth and poverty, truth and tolerance—that have troubled nations and their leaders over the centuries gives students a perspective on the ways in which current leaders are looking at the world, and provides a framework for choosing among candidates and issues.

Familiarity with the United States—its resources, its form of government, its institutions, the diversity of its people and environment—is indispensable. Town and state governments are easily accessible to children in the earlier grades, and each state and each town is likely to be seen as grappling with a dilemma that provides a perfect case study. At what point does a government infringe on the rights and choices of others? What are the rights of minorities? Should water from a nearby river be diverted to supply a distant city? At what cost? Who should decide whether a developer can build a mall on existing farm land? The early grades are not too early to learn about some of the compromises that are part of our political system.

Social studies, like many subjects discussed in this book, is one to which a student returns again and again, each time bringing a new perspective and acquiring a new level of mastery. With each progression, material is presented and understood with greater sophistication, incorporating earlier knowledge as well as new work in other areas.

Several teaching approaches can be considered. A class can focus on one country and, over the course of a year or a semester, learn about the physical and social geography, the culture and customs of the people, and the nature of government. This approach is one we recommend especially in the early years.

This second approach is more a departmental understanding. It focuses on the physical aspects of the environment, the ways in which they affect man at one extreme, and the nature of social institutions—from the family to religious organizations and governments—at the other. This approach is more suited to the later years.

We envision a plan of study beginning in kindergarten and continuing through high school that includes much of what is called geography in the European curriculum and the best of what is now a part of the social studies curriculum in schools in the United States, both in their historical context.

## THE LOWER AND MIDDLE GRADES

In the early and middle grades of primary school, the social component of learning is mainly anecdotal, dealing with personalities and adventures likely to capture the children's imagination. Only a rudimentary attempt is made to present a coherent framework for the ancient world or the present. But even this modest introduction to social studies may develop the child's ability to distinguish the various aspects of social life.

Children's literature, for example, often pictures a medieval fair. The questions raised by such a subject can be endlessly engaging. What was a fair? What was bought or bartered there, and where did it all come from? What kinds of people would be there? How could you tell them apart? The priest, the nun, the count and countess, the merchant and the peasant—what did they do and what was expected of them? Who protected the fair grounds and saw that the people were not robbed? What would happen to a robber who was caught? What would all those kinds of people do for amusement, when they were not working?

In the primary grades, family history may also be used as a starting point for the study of important questions. There the child's first notion of "other times" is stirred. The study of one's family provides a natural opportunity to pose "social studies" questions about life for grandfather and grandmother and their parents:

What was their "economic" life? How did they feed, clothe and house themselves? How was the work shared? How did the sharing affect the life of the family?

What was their "social" life? What kinds of people were they close to?

Did they always speak English? Did their parents? What country did their own grandparents come from?

What did they do for fun when they were not working? What did they read? What music did they like?

During the early years of school, children can acquire some experience in the gathering of first-hand evidence. From the first grade, children may visit their own town or neighborhood to become aware of different human pursuits related to the physical environment. Soon they may go on to consider the economic basis of local life. How does their own town acquire food, clothing, and shelter? Where are the work places, what are the crafts and professions, the means of production, transportation, and distribution?

Teachers in the early years have repeatedly said that their students learn well when one country or region becomes the focus of study for six weeks. During this time students learn some of the characteristics of a given country and its culture; they locate cities, mountains, rivers, neighboring countries; they draw maps and make tools and objects commonly used in that country; they

127

achieve a sense of the culture through reading literature, preparing meals, acting in plays, and reading history; they can discuss in a rudimentary way the significance of different religions, lifestyles, and political and economic systems.

Almost from the beginning, children want to know about their natural environment: Where does the water in the nearby river come from? How did it get there? When children first learn that theirs is not the only way of life, they yearn for information about others. Why don't the Russians write the way we do? If we don't write the same way, why do we have some of the same fairy tales?

For a young American, one way to perceive the relationship between people and their environment is through the study of Indian tribes that have inhabited this country. The way of life of the Apache hunters was different from the Navajo farmers; the precautions that a Seminole takes to protect himself in his hot climate are different from those of the Eskimo. Because animals and crops vary from region to region, diets and customs of food preparation differ. A second grader can think of many questions about man's adaptation to his environment and explore the circumstantial roots of cultural differences—questions that will be asked with greater sophistication at a later age.

In the early grades, students can also examine the methods we use to learn about other cultures—from oral history to archeology—and speculate what the 30th century's archeologists will think of our way of life. The students may explore the social, economic, and cultural life of their town by means of interview and questionnaires. They may learn to use the tools of the social scientist: photographs, slides, films, and tapes; maps, charts, graphs; objects and documents originating in the past. Of course, the interviews and questionnaires, as well as field trips, learning aids, artifacts, and documents should be used in such a way as to reflect questions raised by the children themselves.

128

Children at the lower level should also acquire basic facts about places—where places are and what they are like. A third grader should be able to go to a map and identify most of the nations of the world and every state in the United States. He or she should be able to name the principal cities of the world, including the United States, as well as the great river systems and the major climatic zones of the earth. Third graders should know something of where natural resources occur and should have some appreciation of the natural phenomena that affect all regions: flooding, volcanoes, hurricanes, and earthquakes.

In the upper primary grades, or lower middle school, students may examine more systematically how economic, social, and cultural activities are carried on in other cultures and at other times. At this level, journals and notebooks can be put to good use. Projects can become more ambitious, bringing history, geography, and social studies together, as in a study of the changing modes of transport and travel in a given region, some readings on the relations between climate, terrain, resources, and work, or a discussion of invention, technology, and production.

The upper primary grades are also the time to explore our nation as a whole, and its place in the world. The study of population trends, both contemporary and historical, may introduce a consideration of numbers, distribution, density, composition by race, language, religion, age, sex, and level of education. Students may learn something of economic sectors and social stratification in the United States: they may distinguish agricultural and industrial areas, perceive the networks of transportation and communication that exist, and note some of the public services and social programs to which they are entitled; they should also begin to recognize the media that pervade their lives.

By the seventh grade, students should be devoting seminar time to discussion of original works that introduce them to the principles of U.S. government and citizenship: *The Declaration of Independence,* selections from Tocqueville, Washington's *Farewell Address,* and other significant documents. These seventh grade seminars will be preparation for more detailed and complete seminars that become a part of the curriculum in higher grades. (Consult the Appendix for other documents that should be read by every student.)

## THE UPPER GRADES

It is imperative that the social studies curriculum in the upper grades, through what is now called high school, be designed in direct relation to what has been offered before. New subject areas should not be introduced abruptly. Nor should earlier subjects merely be repeated in greater detail; rather, they must be reexamined in the light of new and more sophisticated questions.

The methods of teaching are the same as those used in the early years. Maps, movies, and books should be used to aid in the transfer of information, the development of skills, and the consideration of major problems. Seminars have a much more prominent place in the curriculum. The master subjects of history and geography touch increasingly upon economic, social, political, and cultural matters. Instruction in government and citizenship becomes more challenging, and the insights of social studies are applied more systematically than at first to the examination of life in other parts of the world.

It is not our intention to produce a detailed syllabus. But a number of topics that might be pursued in historical context suggest themselves: the voyages of discovery and European expansion, the evolution of agriculture and mining, banking and navigation, the application of science and invention, the Industrial Revolution, the evolution of modern class structures, the impact

130

of war on world economics, depression and its sources, the movement of peoples, urbanization, the rise of various economic and social movements and ideologies, 20th century technologies and the nuclear revolution in particular, the relationship between technology and culture—these are some of the matters that may be taken up.

Other possible topics for consideration in the upper grades are: demography, economic growth and its impact, relations between developed and underdeveloped nations, the economic systems of major states and regions of the world, the effects of technology on modern life, international trade and production, and problems of resources, energy, and ecology. These phenomena are to be found in each of the major world areas—the Americas, Europe, the Middle East, India, China and Japan, Africa, the Soviet Union, and Central Asia—to varying extents.

Special attention should be given to at least one non-Western region or nation. The scope of such a study should be thorough, building on foundations laid in the shorter units presented in elementary school. It is at this point that students will do more than identify the relationship between climate, resources, and political and economic systems within a particular culture. They will go on to grasp a central fact: people with societal rules that appear irrational to us can have internally consistent systems of customs and beliefs—which is not to say that all such systems are equally reasonable or equally good.

One unit should be devoted to understanding the United States in some detail: the demographic, economic, and social features of the country that give it its current character and create its current problems: how decisions are made in Washington; the working of the constitution; the making of laws; the administrative departments; the role of the courts. Differences among regions, the role of immigrants, income distribution, the effect of special interests, and the ways in which change can take place in our society are all important subjects for study.

As part of the program in the upper years, regular seminar readings should be chosen with concern for the ideas that shape nations and governments. In these seminars different meanings of such ideas as liberty, equality, justice, citizenship, democracy, tyranny, despotism, constitutional government, and law may have to be explored. The Bill of Rights provides ample background for a discussion of civil liberties, including freedom of speech.

Other subjects for the upper grades are the rights of minorities in a democracy governed by a system of majority rule; the relationship between individuals, the community, and the nation; and the obligation of governments to ensure that basic human needs are met. By no means all of the questions to which these matters give rise can be considered, of course, but some are of great importance. Students should study the revolutions that have occurred in our time and consider how they have influenced the ways in which people think about politics and government. Complex questions arise pertaining to contemporary life, especially in the United States. How, for example, has the introduction of nuclear weapons changed the way our democracy works? How is public opinion formed and what is its role? What is the relationship between experts and well-informed voters? How should we evaluate all the information that is now available to us?

Among these subjects, none could more effectively be used to demonstrate the need for an interdisciplinary approach than that of nuclear power in peace and war. A single, well-chosen book for a Column Three seminar would make it obvious that the insights of history, geography, the social studies, government and civics, science and literature are all necessary to explore the dimensions of this latest human adventure. No answer to the underlying questions may appear. But it is not beyond the capacity of high

132

school students to realize that some things are worth learning, some questions worth struggling over, simply because human dignity calls upon us to be conscious of who we are and what is happening to us. Certainly older students can learn that what sets us apart from the rest of nature is our ability to reflect upon where we have come from and what we have done, and to understand the implications of our actions.

A.S. & P.G.

# 9
# A FOREIGN LANGUAGE

## THE TWO PURPOSES TO BE SERVED
## BY THE STUDY OF A FOREIGN LANGUAGE
## IN A PAIDEIA SCHOOL

THE STUDY of a foreign language is a requirement in a Paideia school, where the foreign language program is a counterpart to the English language and literature program. The choice of which modern (or, perhaps, ancient) language is to be studied is left to the individual school. As it is desirable to have community support within the school for such study, one foreign language should be agreed upon, or—if the school is very large—at most two or three languages should be offered from among which students can choose.

The Paideia foreign language program has two main purposes. One is to enhance language skills in general, and to promote a better understanding of language, again in general. The first beneficiary of this greater skill in language is, of course, the English language program. Students who, through their study of a foreign language, come to understand better the mechanisms and processes of language in general are likely to be more skilled in using their own language.

The other main purpose is to expand the cultural experience of students and beyond that of their immediate linguistic group. The

134

study of a foreign language in connection with the culture it both expresses and reflects is one way to avoid cultural provincialism.

Several other purposes or objectives are served by the study of a foreign language, but these do not fall within the curricular framework and aims of a Paideia school. Thus, in the Three Column diagram on page 8, the study of a foreign language is not mentioned, since it is subordinate to the development of general language skills, on the one hand, and to the study of geography and other cultures, on the other.

Among these other purposes or objectives that the study of a foreign language serves are the following:

(a) making use of language for travel or commerce. The advantages of knowing and being able to use a foreign language are obvious to anyone who undertakes travel abroad or engages in international business, but these are likely to be only a minority of the students in their years of basic schooling;

(b) doing advanced work in a foreign language, including the study of the major literary works in that language. Again, this applies only to a minority;

(c) enjoying the satisfaction of reading, speaking, and thinking in a second language, even if this language is not used for travel or business and even if it does not become a field of further study. Effective command of another language— bilingualism—is a source of pleasure, as everybody knows, but again, this is likely to occur or be possible for only a minority of students in basic schooling.

Such purposes and objectives, and others as well, have intrinsic merit or appeal, either for their own sake or for one or another utilitarian reason. Students motivated by such interests or appeals may go further in their study of a foreign language, either

135

on their own, in association with other students in a "language club," or with some form of outside help (that is, outside of the Paideia school). Further study is, of course, open to students in college, graduate school, or elsewhere.

However, within the framework of the Paideia Program the educational significance of foreign-language study is thought by a majority of the Paideia Group to be limited to the two main purposes stated above.


## HOW THESE TWO PURPOSES ARE TO BE SERVED

In a Paideia school, the foreign language program is divided, more or less sharply, into two parts, which occur at different times during the course of basic schooling. Both parts of the program serve the main purposes described in the first section of this chapter, but in different ways. Both are chiefly Column Two activities.

*The early years.* Beginning in the early years of schooling, frequent periods of coaching and frequent opportunities to exercise language skills are desirable for all students (see the discussion of early English language study in Chapter 4). The very early years of a child's life are best for learning to speak and understand a foreign language, so far as the Paideia requirement goes. At this period of their lives it is not difficult for children to acquire such skills, though they may not yet be able to read and write even their own language. A second language at this time is an exciting and gratifying accomplishment for them, and the speed with which they acquire competence serves both to heighten their interest and to increase their self-esteem.

The emphasis in the early years should be on informal conversation, stories, songs, and plays—activities that keep the experience enjoyable. Consideration should be given to having one of the early years a year in which parts of the whole curriculum are taught in a second language. Children might then perceive all of the different subjects they know or have heard about exist in the second language, making the important point that all of life is lived by other peoples, each in its own language. The extent to which those school subjects are mastered in the second language is of less importance than the realization of that general fact.

During this year, the children can be introduced to various aspects of the foreign culture by all members of the teaching staff that speak the second language. The experience of pretending to be a member of that culture is of lasting benefit to children for the reason given above.

*Coaching.* Coaching is central to successful language teaching and learning, whether the skill desired is in one's native language or a foreign one. For the student to learn, and not merely go through pointless exercises, all the skills must grow together— listening, speaking, reading, and writing. Ways and means of coaching language will be found in both Chapter 2, "Coaching" and Chapter 4, "English Language and Literature." The methods and practices that work for English will work with French or any other tongue. The one notable difference is that in beginning the study of a foreign language, greater emphasis must be laid on listening and speaking. This is to make up for the head start that the child has with respect to his native language.

Of the two methods of teaching foreign languages—one in which English is spoken much of the time; the other in which little or no English is spoken—many teachers have found astoundingly better results with the second. This is particularly true with young children, because they like making and listening to sounds even when these carry little or no meaning, because they feel freer than adults about guessing meanings and responses. After all, that is what they have been doing in order to learn their own language.

137

Accordingly, in the early years of schooling in a foreign language, frequent, intense periods of coaching and frequent opportunities to talk are vital.

*The later years.* In the later years, after some skill in using the foreign language has been acquired, a foreign language becomes an object of formal study. Analysis of its grammar and linguistic structures, the study of its literature, and the introduction of problems of translation, which are complex and difficult, increase the understanding that has already been acquired through conversational skills. The aim at this stage is to enhance the understanding of English, which by then the child should know how to read, write, and speak capably. At the same time, coaching and didactic teaching begin to connect the language with the social institutions of the foreign country. The value of studying the language and its associated culture together is self-evident.

At both stages of the program, several side benefits accrue. Most important is the deepening of perception in the study of English literature and its language. Students come to understand what language essentially is: a largely arbitrary means of communicating. It is a revelation to many students to learn that foreigners speak about the same things that they speak about, have the same hopes, fears, desires, but use entirely different words to express them. This is an insight conducive not only to the reduction of cultural provincialism, but also to the appreciation of mankind's linguistic powers.

At the same time, the student discovers that no language, even our own, is a complete and wholly flexible incarnation of our thoughts. Certain ideas have found expression in French, for example, that are, if not impossible, then much more difficult to express in English, and vice versa. The same goes for any other pair of languages; and between the members of some pairs—English and Japanese, for instance—there is less accommodation than be-

138

tween members of pairs of "neighboring" languages. Language, in short, while the best means of communication that human beings have, is also an obstacle to communication, when that word means shared understanding of ideas and values.

## THE TIME TO BE DEVOTED TO FOREIGN LANGUAGE STUDY

The view that has prevailed with the majority of the Paideia Group calls for at least four years of study of a foreign language by all students and allows for the extension of the program to six years of study by all students wherever a school finds it expedient.

How the time allotted for foreign language study is to be divided between the two parts of the program will be decided by a Paideia school itself. If the total years scheduled for is six, then three years (or four) may be devoted to the foreign language in the lower school, leaving two (or three) years of more formal study of grammar and literature for the upper school. If the total time is four years, then this may be divided two and two. The Paideia Group believes that in the upper grades a second foreign language can be appropriately substituted for the first, particularly if the second is Latin or Greek, in which conversational ability is not required.

Older children, who will have acquired some conversational ability in the first foreign language, may be able to coach the younger ones, affording a satisfying experience for both. In addition, after four years (or six) of exposure to a foreign language, many students should be able to overcome the frustrations that arise from spending too little time on a language, or not enough in a concentrated span, which makes virtually impossible the kind of competence that makes language study gratifying.

Since the emphasis in the later years is on grammar, vocabulary, and syntax, and the major tasks will be the translation of written materials from one language to another, it is not necessary that conversational ability be achieved in a second foreign language. Indeed, if the second language is Latin or Greek, oral communication will not be an objective.

G.V.D. & C.V.D.

# 10
## The Fine Arts

A READING of *The Paideia Proposal* will show that the conception of man as an artist (woman, too), as one who knows how to do things, is fundamental to it. The program envisions the active participation of children, throughout their basic schooling, in every kind of art appropriate to their stage of development. It may be argued that first in importance among the skills or arts to be acquired are the traditional liberal ones—the verbal and mathematical skills we use to understand the world around us in its qualitative and its quantitative aspects. But these arts are merely part of a series that includes at once the useful arts, in which the aim is not understanding but application, and the fine arts, in which the aim is the rendering of certain aspects of human experience for its own sake, valued for its own perfection.

This characteristic of the fine arts—their lack of any purpose save their own realization and the interest we take in it—has sometimes caused them to be regarded not only as less important than the other arts, but as altogether superfluous, even frivolous activities. That is not our view, nor do we think of them merely as embellishments, a graceful addition to the meat and potatoes of basic schooling. On the contrary, we regard such arts as serv-

141

ing real human needs—for self-expression to begin with, and for the account they provide of the world we find about and within us (an account no less true, though in detail very different, from the one that science affords). No creature but man is capable of the fine arts, while man has never, or only in rare instances, been willing to exist without them. Hence the place we have made for them in our Paideia curriculum, both as something to know and as something we ought in some measure to be able to do.

We think also that the fine arts cannot be omitted from the course of study, or short-changed in it, without damage to all the other arts. History tells us what happens when one or another part of the series is lost or neglected. What happens is that the remaining arts become either swollen or enfeebled. Without the liberal arts to give purpose to them, the useful arts explode into runaway techniques—that is, technology. Without those same liberal arts, which enable them to illuminate human experience, the fine arts become dilettantish or obscure, occupied with empty gestures. Without application or propriety, such as the useful and fine arts respectively can teach, the liberal arts themselves degenerate, becoming dull exercises for pedants or dangerous propaganda for fanatics. *The Paideia Program* means to avoid these perversions, assuming that none of them can be fended off unless all are, which is to say unless each of the kinds of art is given its due.


WHICH FINE ARTS?

The fine arts we recommend for inclusion in the curriculum are music, drama, dance, drawing, painting, sculpture (or modeling), and crafts. Of these, the first three can be characterized as symbolic arts because they consist variously of notes, figures, and words, which require the student to engage in interpretation and expression. The last four may be characterized as material arts, meaning that what is required is to make or transform some material thing; the activity of the students involves working with the material and discovering how and to what ends it can be handled.

In using these terms, we do not imply that the first group of arts does not make use of the creative imagination. Often it does. In dance, the activity may express an idea figured in the students' own movements. In music and dramatic performance, the composition or the play may be interpreted so as to constitute something original. Nor do we wish to imply that the material arts listed above are not themselves expressions of meaning—even, certainly, the student artist's meaning in symbolic form. Of course they are such expressions, and of course what is expressed in already existing models—the paintings and drawings and works of sculpture by the masters—is a proper subject of study and discussion, quite as much as are plays and musical compositions.

Nevertheless, the distinction is real between a group of arts in which what is to be dealt with is *always* a set of symbols, whether given or invented, and one in which what is to be dealt with is *always* a tangible object, whether drawn from purely imaginative sources or constructed to represent some other object already existing—as is the case, for example, with a portrait. The distinction is real, and it derives from the fact that the arts in the first group are related to the traditional liberal arts, which they overlap. For example, in drama, the play as a text is a work of literature, while as a production it is a work of dramatic art. The arts in the second group, which we have called material arts, stand closer to the useful arts, which they also overlap. For example, what are called crafts include things produced for use, such as a piece of clothing or furniture. These different origins and purposes for the two groups

143

of fine arts mean that some can be effectively taught and learned with the related liberal arts, others with the related useful arts.

## THE DIRECTION AND SCOPE OF FINE ARTS TEACHING

The program we envision will be determined to some extent by the nature of the various arts themselves. As the liberal arts have their source in the intellect, and the useful arts in the structure of our bodies, of which tools are an extension, so the fine arts take their rise in our perceptions, through which we put ourselves in touch with our surroundings. "All men by nature desire to know," runs a famous statement by Aristotle, who adds that "an indication of this is the delight they take in their senses." This delight is inborn and therefore capable of development in very young children. Indeed, the fine arts are the first ones that can be attempted by the young, who before they know how to make effective use of tools, or even of their minds, are able to use their eyes and ears and fingers to explore whatever lies about them.

At first this exploration is and should be unrestrained, free to go in any direction not positively destructive that it likes. To start too early to put limits on it, to try to train it, is a mistake. Children have a natural love of art and are wonderfully inventive and imaginative in their expression of it. Not only should we give this expression free rein for a while, we should pay attention to what it produces and encourage further efforts.

But it is also an error to let random exploration go too far. Endeavor in the arts "is not all passion and vitality," as Jerome Bruner says: "There is a decorum in creative activity, a love of form, an etiquette toward the object of our efforts, a respect for materials." And just as unfortunate as children who have not been allowed to be free are those who have never been taught to be anything else. Such are children too old for untrained expression, children

144

who, if they are not disheartened by their sense of what they cannot effectively or gracefully do, are at any rate sadly incompetent in their attempts to do it.

The same progression which the liberal and useful arts take through the school years should be followed by the fine arts. The progression is from the student to the subject, from attention to the child to attention to what the child is doing or learning. In the fine arts, as elsewhere, this progression should be gradual, and the sense of what pace is proper may vary with the child, the teacher, the school, and each art itself. It is "a subtle matter of timing," Bruner notes: "when the impulse, when the taming." But a progression should occur lest the practice of arts wither from a perception (which the child quickly learns) that they are not taken seriously, that the mere attempt is enough.

This does not mean that the aim of the fine arts program is to turn out painters or poets or actors or dancers in any finished, professional sense of those terms. In a Paideia school that would be quite as wrong as to imagine that through the liberal arts such a school can produce mathematicians and historians, or by the useful arts it can train carpenters, cooks, and mechanics. The aim of schooling to enable those who undergo it to become their own teachers—which is to say, those who know how to learn by themselves. *The Paideia Proposal* says there ought to be sufficient competence in *all* the arts—useful and fine, as well as liberal—for continued learning and practice to go on. That is far from the mastery required for performance or production in the fine arts, which would pervert the Paideia schooling if it were attempted. But it is also far from the awkwardness, the ignorance, the inarticulateness with respect to such arts which is to be found among the larger part of the school population today.

Can something between these extremes be achieved consistent with the other demands of the curriculum, manageable without excessive amounts of time or money having to be spent? We think it can. We think it will be sufficient, broadly speaking, if regular but informal attention is paid in the lower grades to guided practice in the fine arts, which will insure the learning of certain basic skills. Again, it will be sufficient if, in the upper grades, approximately three years of at least weekly classes are also devoted to each of the two kinds of art we have distinguished. We assume that exercises in the lower grades are for the most part within the competence of the regular grade teachers, while exercises in the upper grades should be supervised by experienced fine arts teachers.

The scheme of a Paideia fine arts program might look approximately as follows, much being left to the invention of individual teachers, particularly in the lower grades:

### GRADES K TO 5 OR 6

| | |
|---|---|
| Music: | group singing and recorder playing |
| Dramatics: | class plays—reading and production |
| Dance: | rhythmic movement, simple exercises, folk dancing |
| Drawing & Painting: | both informal, but using as good materials as possible |
| Modeling: | objects in Plasticine or clay pottery |
| Crafts: | simple things of wood or other convenient material, textile, etc. |

### GRADES 6 OR 7 TO 12

| | |
|---|---|
| Music: | 2 years, one of chorus, one of listening to and discussing good music |

146

| | |
|---|---|
| Drama & Dance: | a half year to each, ending in one substantial play, one group dance for the grade peers |
| Drawing & Painting: | 1 year of composition and design, with basic instruction in colors |
| Modeling & Crafts: | 1 year ending with an exhibit of some work by each child |
| Masterworks: | 1 year's observation and discussion of great works of art, including trips to museums, study of art books, slides, etc. |

Such a scheme is adequate, we believe, *provided* that all children in the lower grades are taught to read music and to play the recorder, a cheap instrument, easy to learn, for which much good music can be transcribed (a few introductory lessons by an experienced music teacher may be called for); *provided also* that care is taken to note the age at which a given child's development allows instruction in drawing and the kind of "seeing" it requires—an age beyond which such a child should not be left simply to scratch and dabble; and *provided finally* that throughout good music and drama are selected for study and practice, and good materials (not necessarily expensive) are available to those who draw, paint, and model. Theme songs from movies and blunt wax crayons have very little instructional value.

If the demands of such a program on school time appear too great, portions of it may perhaps be combined with other parts of the curriculum. Indeed, some coordination is desirable, for all forms of expression are related and should seem to be. The fine arts program, which has a tendency to become specialized, should be as fully integrated as possible with the work in the liberal arts and in the useful ones. This adjustment will keep the fine arts from using up too much "extra" time.

Should anybody wonder what a class in mathematics can have to do with painting, let Cezanne's remark be recalled when he said that the painter sees all objects in terms of their geometry. In music, anyone can hear the intervals and learn from the physics of sound how deviations from strict ratios has permitted what we call harmony. So with other subjects such as history and language. Students who are reading *Hamlet* should take it for granted that their schooling will extend from reading the play to speaking it aloud, seeing it performed, acting in it, and possibly giving time to making scenery for its production. Students who are learning carpentry should have some sense of the form, some grasp of the aesthetics of manufactured things; they should also know the abstract function of the tools they use and their underlying principles. As for dance practice, especially for boys, it will be more acceptable if it takes place in the gymnasium and is shown as a strenuous part of physical education.

Allowance must, of course, be made for individual cases of special awkwardness or disability. The very few children who are truly tone deaf should not be forced to sing; those with physical handicaps should not be forced to dance. But with sympathetic instruction, these exceptions will prove far less common than is usually supposed. The help of an experienced arts teacher is especially valuable to such children; it may rescue them from an imaginary—or at least remediable—incapacity.

## THE THREE KINDS OF TEACHING IN THE FINE ARTS

Any fine arts program is largely a matter of coaching, of developing certain skills under guidance. Most of the hours the student spends at fine arts in a Paideia school will be hours of exercise and practice. Consequently, the work is not "teacher intensive." A competent music teacher can instruct several choruses or instrumental groups, and so can the teacher of dance or the teacher of dramatics. Even in the material arts, where students work individually and require individual attention, it need not be always close attention. A word now and then, an observation here and there, is often all that is required, and a skilled teacher can help many children at one time. This does not justify overloading the fine arts staff, which must be able to meet the students' needs, especially the needs of those youngsters who find it harder than do others to keep time, to make the right movements, to mix paints, and so forth.

There is, however, a Column Three aspect to such a program as well—one which, though fewer hours need to be devoted to it, is as important as the actual practice of the various arts. The Column Three aspect of the program is the experience and discussion of good music and good works of graphic and modeled art—at least a year of each—which should be required of all students. This will occur in seminars of a kind, the kind being one in which the subject will often be something either played or displayed, as the case may be, at the time of discussion, or just before.

It is of the first importance that all students participate in this talk, not as a way to "learn the subject," but in order to see that insights into works of art are really possible, can be arrived at, articulated, and improved by being made explicit. What is sought is full awareness and an intelligent response, the ability to see and hear with discrimination, lest we be blind and deaf to what goes on in the arts and artifacts, good or bad, that are everywhere around us. The students' own experience in the practice of the arts must of course be brought to bear on the subject of the discussion.

For "intelligent response," information is also required, beyond what either coaching or seminars can be expected to provide.

Again, this need not be left to the fine arts teachers only. Teachers of other subjects should provide their students with art books, pictures on the class walls, records, plays, trips to museums, and the study of tools, machinery, buildings, and gardens. In particular, children studying history should know that art and artists have played a great role in the past, that particular works have historical significance—witness Beethoven's "Eroica" symphony and the French Revolution, or the Gothic cathedrals and medieval Christendom. American art and architecture can be found in many parts of the country to accompany the study of the national past, while photographs and films will be good substitutes elsewhere. Such exposure will constitute the Column One contribution to the fine arts program. It should leave the older students with some sense of what the main epochs of art have been and what works and great figures belong to each.

## RIGHT AND WRONG ATTITUDES

In some schools the attitude toward the fine arts may be so skeptical that their role in the curriculum to the extent here recommended will be threatened. If skepticism results in inadequate funding and poor staffing, there will be no way to remedy it. Yet the fear of expense is often a poor excuse; a good arts program need cost no more than an elective program does in schools as they are now. Nor is that the one problem. Even if money and staff are provided, there may be opposition to the program on other grounds from children and their parents.

This opposition may arise from antagonism based on the belief that the fine arts have no market value. In that case it will not be much different from what is likely to be felt about many aspects of Paideia schooling by those who wish no more for their children than an immediate paying job. The response must be a patient explanation of Paideia's three lifetime objectives, among which the making of a good human life for oneself is more important even than that of good citizenship and the capacity to earn a living. And what needs to be emphasized is that the first of these objectives cannot be achieved unless the fine arts play a part in it. This they do whether we like it or not. Common to all our lives are rhythms, voices, and objects and structures of every sort—our man-made surroundings. But too many adults lack the knowledge and confidence with which to judge the worth of what clutters up their environment. They are thus limited to the choices that pop culture, mass production, and manipulative media put before them.

In addition, some children and their parents will have cultural backgrounds that make a particular fine arts program seem alien or unintelligible, even if they are well-disposed toward it. When that is so, efforts must be made to keep activities simple, at least in the beginning, and to include among them artistic achievements from the ethnic and cultural background of the school population. This is not to forget that our cultural heritage is predominantly Western and European. It is, and any Paideia fine arts program must reflect the fact. But it does not follow that only Mozart and Michelangelo belong in such a program, however important it may be to recognize such names. The good fine arts teacher will remember that there is great art also in Africa, in Asia, and in Central and South America, and will make sure that children become aware of it.

Whatever else is done, attention must be paid to the school's own physical appearance and environment. Not all schools need improvement in this respect, but most do, and some are desperate cases. It is asking a lot of children to expect them to know good music, color, and design when their surroundings are barren, ugly, and uninviting, and when the only notes they ever hear are those of Muzak, hit songs, and cafeteria din. They can at least be provided with well-painted corridors, attractively arranged rooms, exhibits of art arranged at many points with proper lighting, and performances by such musicians as those of Young Audiences whenever the schedule permits.

The help of parents and artists in the neighborhood can be employed in this upgrading of the visual and auditory environment. Volunteer help of many kinds is often available for fine arts programs, and should be made use of. The school then becomes a place of interest to people of talent in the community, people whose encouragement and support will make not only its fine arts program but the whole Paideia undertaking easier than it would otherwise be.

And still, when all is said and done and every effort has been made, there will be children and their parents—and school boards and state legislatures—who will ask what good the fine arts program really does, why time and money should be devoted to it. The answer to this is no harder and no easier to come by than when the question is asked about other aspects of Paideia schooling, such as mathematics or a foreign language, which some people think superfluous. The answer is that the possession of such knowledge will prepare the individual for whatever challenge society confronts him or her with. In addition to which, the trained mind is better able to keep its balance in a bewildering world and enjoy what good it has to offer. Both are among the conditions of human freedom. Human beings are not free without some real sense of their environment and some power to design their lives; they are prisoners of fear, incompetence, and ignorance—easy prey for the bigot, the exploiter, and the tyrant who may at any time appear. A well-schooled population, aware of its human capacities and proud of its human distinction, is the best defense against such evils, indeed the only defense that in the long run has any chance of success. It is for the sake of such a chance, and from a belief in its importance—for everybody—that Paideia schooling, in all its aspects, has been conceived.

J.V.D.

# 11
## The Manual Arts

THE PAIDEIA CURRICULUM does not include vocational training for a well-considered reason. The first twelve years of schooling is the inappropriate time—and school is the inappropriate place—for learning marketable skills. The time for learning these technical skills is after basic education has been completed, as we explain in the subsequent chapter. But this conclusion must not be misunderstood: our objection is to specific job training, and not to general education in the manual arts. Hence, we do not advocate boarding-up the woodshops, typing rooms, and other workplace classrooms in the nation's schools. On the contrary, that which is taught at present in these facilities could be readily modified and turned into practical, truly educational courses. Indeed, we believe that such courses should be required of all students—irrespective of their sex, career interests, or innate abilities.

But it is important for teachers and parents to remember that the teaching of crafts, mechanics, and the domestic arts is justifiable only as a contribution to learning, rather than as a direct preparation for future employment. This is true even if such general training improves the student's capacities in many lines of adult work. Acquiring skill in the manual arts is as much mind-training as acquiring skill in the language arts.

After going through the Paideia Program, all young people should be familiar with the handling of basic tools and machines; all should be able to make simple, useful objects from wood and other common materials; and all should be able to make elementary repairs on household devices.

Clearly, the young man who cannot cook his own dinner, the young woman who does not understand the function of a car generator, the young person who does not know how to wire a light-switch are all at a considerable disadvantage in life. In the lower schools, young children can be taught to use common tools, to hammer a nail, saw a straight cut, sew on a button, or hem a garment. Beginning about age twelve or thirteen, and continuing throughout the last five or six years of basic schooling, students might be taught such things as how to replace a spark plug, change a tire, bake a cake, prepare a hot breakfast, and make simple repairs of home plumbing and electrical systems.

This list is merely illustrative. Any common skill that can be used by all in whatever careers they choose would be similarly appropriate. Certainly, safety (electricity, fire, protecting the eyes) and the care of tools (sharpening knives, handling electric saws) should be part of the school curriculum. A knowledge of the principles of tools can also serve as an excellent introduction to the physical sciences ("Why is a crowbar shaped the way it is?" "What is the physical principle behind the wrench?"). Besides, making things is a natural way to develop an understanding of proportion and other mathematical concepts, as well as of the relationship of form and function, which is a pedagogical link to the fine arts.

In addition to the obvious usefulness of the manual arts, the making of things brings its own satisfactions. One should learn to make things as the basis for appreciation of what is involved in anything that is well made. In the not distant future, high quality goods, services, and ideas will be America's most important product.

The central consideration is that whatever is taught should be a skill that will be needed by everyone in the brave, new post-industrial world. Typing is a prime example of such a skill. Because of the growing use of computers the ability to type will be required of everybody in school, at home, and on the job. It should clearly be the first manual skill taught. Age eight is not too young to begin, and since most children will have been playing with computer keyboards beginning in kindergarten, it may be impossible to hold them back from formal training until age eight!

How should these skills be taught? By coaching: there is no other way to learn them; they can be acquired only by doing, under the watchful eye of a patient coach.

Who should teach them? Ideally, they should be taught by members of the regular academic faculty and not by specialists. This would facilitate the integration of concepts from mathematics, economics, physics, and other relevant disciplines, as well as prevent invidious distinctions from arising among the faculty.

How much time should be devoted to the manual arts? An hour to two a week for three or more years should provide adequate time and exposure without greatly disrupting the inner-balance of the curriculum.

J.O'T.

# 12
## The World of Work

OURS IS AN ADVANCED, post-industrial economy in which machines are coming to do most of society's *labor*. Most of the *work* that will remain will be good work—work that requires human intelligence, not animal strength.

In such an economy, the skills of reading, writing, speaking, listening, observing, measuring, and calculating are essential preparations for any job youth may want to pursue in the future. In the fast changing world in which specific vocational training will be quickly outmoded by technological, economic, and social advances, the only appropriate "career education" is *learning how to learn*, so that one can quickly prepare for new jobs and career opportunities as they come along. As Robert M. Hutchins once wrote:

> If I had a single message for the younger generation I would say, "Get ready for anything, because anything is what's going to happen." We don't know what it is, and it's very likely that whatever it is won't be what we now think it is.

Since *The Paideia Program* offers the only practical preparation for such an unpredictable future, the general course of study we advocate is the right preparation for the vocations common to all: citizenship, the pursuits of leisure, *and* earning a living.

As the industries supplying services and information come to dominate the American economy, professional, technical, clerical, managerial, and other service occupations will engage the vast majority of young Americans who enter the labor market. Many jobs now require, or will soon require, advanced schooling. The existing institutions of higher education are equipped to provide this advanced professional, managerial, and technical education. Indeed, it is the kind of schooling most of these institutions are best equipped to provide. It is fast becoming the only kind of schooling that highly specialized faculties are willing to provide. The existing system of higher education is thus already geared to the *advanced* preparation for work that will be its prime responsibility as soon as *general* education is recognized as the responsibility of basic schooling.

There will, of course, be many graduates of Paideia schools who will not wish to pursue advanced training. It is therefore essential that vocational training should be available to them at cost-free public institutions, *after* they graduate from basic schooling. These institutions would be staffed by the vocational teachers in the existing high schools and community colleges, thus preventing severe dislocations for vocational teachers or institutions.

The eighteen-year-olds who voluntarily choose to enter vocational training will be qualitatively different from today's vocational students: *they will have had an excellent general education.* This will better serve the ends of equality than any form of vocational education ever tried. Differences among social groups will be greatly reduced when all eighteen-year-olds will have had the same preparation. Differences in occupations will remain, but differences in opportunity, class, and culture will be much less. Vocational educators will then have a more satisfying role and they will not be forced to do remedial teaching. Instead, they will be free to do what they are best prepared to do and most interested in doing: technical training and coaching.

158

As explained in Chapter 11, training in the useful arts and crafts is offered in the first twelve years of Paideia schooling, but we believe nonetheless that there is a need for a bridge between schooling and the working world all students will enter. Most pressingly, this bridge is needed to help adolescents understand the nature of the world of work, which includes the career choices they will have to face. Consequently, consideration should be given to providing all students in the twelfth (last year) of basic schooling with some kind of work-and-study experience.

This experience might range from volunteer work in a hospital, to part-time paid work in a factory, office, newspaper, or government bureau, to participation in Junior Achievement. What is fundamental is that young people come to understand through experience both the necessity for work and its responsibilities—the attitudes, habits, constraints and satisfactions inseparable from employment. Hundreds of thousands of young Americans are currently engaged in such informative activities. In the Paideia curriculum, these activities should entail no time away from class; that is, the time spent working should be after school hours, on weekends, or during the summer months. From such jobs would follow a number of educational advantages.

- They would help to overcome age segregation by allowing students to observe adults at work and, in doing so, to learn what it is like to work all day.
- Students would have the opportunity to overcome stereotypes about people who perform kinds of jobs different from their parents'.
- The jobs would enhance the meaning of school work, because students would see how education actually contributes to workaday life.
- Young people would come to know better what they really like

to do and what they are good at doing, and thus develop clearer career aspirations.

- Most important, the work experience could be used to make classroom discussions of social and economic institutions vivid and individually relevant.

The shortage of such opportunities for work is, of course, a practical limitation to this proposal, which is why we advance it as an option only. But there is, of course, no limit to the number of young people who could be engaged in Junior Achievement activities and, since these are far more readily malleable to educational ends, they may be the preferable alternative.

It should also be remembered that apart from work in the market place, work habits can be formed by school work and homework. Both are real work and differ from jobs only in that they are not paid and that they are done for oneself and not for others. Homework, especially, should serve to develop habits of good work. Increased amounts of homework would reduce the number of hours wasted watching television; and homework carefully corrected and repeated if slovenly done, would introduce young Americans to the routine of hard and exact work to which West European, Japanese, Chinese and Russian youth are accustomed at an early age.

J.O'T.

# 13
## Physical Education

THERE CAN BE no argument against physical education for normal, healthy boys and girls. The care of the body is not peripheral to life; it is essential. As such, it should be pursued by *all* students, and by all in the same way.

Unfortunately, physical education is too frequently pursued by some students only. And, in the places where it is pursued by all students, it is done in a differentiated manner; that is, one form of physical education may be pursued by boys, another by girls, one by the athletic and another by the less robust. We think undifferentiated physical education is as important as undifferentiated academic subjects.

During the twelve years of basic schooling, physical training should have two purposes: (1) to develop the knowledge and habits requisite for the care of the body throughout life; and (2) to provide some physical relief from the taxing brain work of schooling.

The second point is in keeping with the tested principle that the mind works best in school or on the job if the body is exercised sometime during the day. Indeed, for young children, exercise breaks are not a luxury; they are a necessity.

These goals are best pursued through programs of exercise and sports that (1) are accessible to all regardless of sex, physical stature, or innate ability, (2) can be pursued throughout one's life after

161

schooling is completed, and (3) do not interfere with the primary purposes of schooling.

Such activities as *intra*mural soccer, cross-country running, swimming, tennis, volleyball, softball, basketball, and other forms of vigorous, organized exercise would meet all these criteria. Interscholastic tackle football would meet none of them. While it is not our intention to advocate the reform of interscholastic sports, it is necessary to call for the reform of sports insofar as they interfere with primary educational goals.

Such interference is manifest. Within recent years, the nation has witnessed the sorry spectacle of boys in their early teens repeating school grades for the sole purpose of putting on weight for football. There is a growing custom in schools and colleges of granting academic credit to athletes for non-academic courses and at times even granting credit for no work at all. In the worst instances, schools and colleges are represented on playing fields not by student-athletes, but by athletes who are students only by virtue of the logos on their jerseys. Too often these disgraceful situations involve athletes from minority groups. These young men pay a high price in later life for having missed their opportunity to become educated.

Such undesirable practices must be eliminated at the level of basic schooling where they do the most harm. The irrelevant pressures created by hypercompetitive sports on school administrators, parents, teachers, coaches, and, worst of all on the athletes themselves, lead to a callous disregard of the basic purpose of schools. We therefore advocate increased emphasis on intramural sports, in which all students can participate, and decreased emphasis on interscholastic competition, in which only a few participate. If anything is elitist, that is it.

Specializing in football, basketball, or baseball with the intent of pursuing a professional career in sports is analogous to vocational training and has no place in basic schooling. Those students who wish to specialize in competitive sports should do so *on their own time, in clubs that have no school affiliation.*

This proposal has ample precedents. High school students today who wish to specialize in opera singing, equestrian sports, roller disco, playing bridge, and the like, must do so on their own time. In Western Europe, athletes are trained in clubs, not in schools. Even in the United States, such high school tennis stars as Tracy Austin and Andrea Jeager did not compete for their schools. It is in the interests of education that football players be treated like bridge players, European soccer players, and American tennis stars. The school playing fields should be opened to *all* students.

We believe, moreover, that it is possible to reconceptualize physical education, creating options for non-competitive exercise. Jogging and swimming need not lead to racing, calisthenics need not lead to competitive gymnastics, and shooting baskets need not lead to traditional basketball games. While competitive sports are fine for many young people, others will be found more willing and better able to engage in exercise if competitiveness is removed or if the competition is with oneself. The growing popularity of such activities as Frisbee, beach paddle ball, aerobic dance, and *t'ai chi* attest to the usefulness of such activities in attracting the natively non-athletic to exercise.

Habits requisite for the care of the body will thus be developed through daily intramural sports or daily stretching, calisthenics, and dance. This requirement is analogous to drilling in other skills. Knowledge about care of the body naturally requires some didactic instruction. Basic schooling should include some knowledge of physiology and anatomy (including sex education), hygiene, and, in this age of lifelong athletics, some introduction to sports medicine to prevent injuries and associated illnesses. These several elements of a physical education program should be distributed appropriately through each of the twelve years of basic schooling.

J.O'T.

# PART THREE
# The Paideia School

# 14
## How a Paideia School Should Be Structured

### THE PROBLEM TO BE SOLVED

WE HAVE been describing the curriculum and its implementation. How should we begin to describe the structure of the school? Because no two Paideia schools are expected to be alike, everything said on the subject must be taken as suggestive or illustrative of general principles. Even so, much can be said about the ways that teaching and learning should be organized to facilitate the realization of its goals. This chapter is written in the belief that any existing school has the capacity to adopt (and adapt) the Paideia curriculum.

There can be no single blueprint for building a Paideia school, no one right model. Yet the public school that implements our curriculum will have certain essential characteristics that will distinguish it from schools as they now exist in the United States. These hallmarks are indicated in earlier chapters of this book, as well as in two earlier books, *The Paideia Proposal* (1982) and *Paideia Problems and Possibilities* (1983). They are summarized again, very briefly, in Chapter 15. In order for the Paideia Program to flourish, existing schools must be restructured.

This restructuring will eliminate much wasteful repetition that now results from uncoordinated programs, not just from week to

167

week or grade to grade, but throughout the years from K through 12.

At present, it is the lower grades that can give us an idea of the basic conditions needed: a manageable number of students for each teacher, a flexible schedule, a limited curriculum, school resources nearby (the library, for example), control of instruction vested in one person. Elementary teachers at this level are mainly generalists, not specialists, and they are responsible for the whole course of study.

In these years, students acquire, through didactic methods (books, telling, movies, records) information and knowledge about science, history, geography, literature, and other Column One subjects. Through coaching they learn to write, read, use numbers, make maps, draw graphs—the Column Two skills. And in some K-3 classrooms today there is a great deal of discussion, of active interchange between teachers and students. Classes often concentrate on broad themes or topics for several weeks—a country or region, an historical period, a people—thus giving coherence to all three kinds of teaching and learning.

## FIRST STEPS TOWARD RESTRUCTURING

The school principal and a group of key teachers must (1) understand the Paideia Proposal, (2) recognize it for the radical idea it is, and (3) be committed to a series of changes that will probably run a decade or more. All three points are prerequisites.

*First,* leadership for adopting the Paideia Program must spring from within a school. The program cannot be successfully imposed by outsiders, although support from central office administrators, school board members, representative parents, and older students are essential. *Second,* without a thorough understanding of the implications of the proposal, school leaders will not be able to restructure the school properly. The American school tends to resist fundamental change and may be expected to be inhospitable. *Third*, the transformation must take place over several years, because it will entail fundamental changes in deeply ingrained ways of thinking about the tasks of schooling and of organizing a school to perform it. Teachers should be ready for a sustained effort. Short bursts of faddish zeal are not likely to accomplish anything.

Readers should refer to Appendix II of *Paideia Problems and Possibilities* for concrete suggestions from school superintendents and principals who have already started to transform existing schools according to Paideia principles. They have reorganized teaching and learning one grade or one subject at a time. Every successful plan will eventually lead to major shifts in four critical areas of operations. These are (1) schedule, (2) deployment of staff, (3) curriculum, and (4) training for the staff. All four factors demand attention from the outset. They are inescapably interdependent. In most cases, it would not be possible to postpone or ignore even one of the four and still create a school faithful to the Paideia Program.

The reason for this can be understood by examining a simple situation. Suppose a secondary school decides to initiate its effort by instituting seminars. The schedule will have to make provision for two-hour periods once or twice every week. Students and staff will have to be organized into groups of 20–25 students with a seminar leader. The curriculum will have to be modified to incorporate Column Three teaching and learning, probably at the expense of Column One. Seminar leaders will have to be trained. Though we can discuss the four factors only one after the other, a school in transition will have to deal with them simultaneously.

SCHEDULES

The typical school week of five identical days, each made up of a series of uniform class periods, imposes a rigid structure on schooling that bears no close relation to the three kinds of teaching and learning that are basic to the Paideia Program. The school schedule must be made flexible enough to suit the character of each subject being studied, the mode of instruction, and the differences in learning ability on the parts of its students.

The centrality and extent of coaching for the Paideia curriculum will be the main cause of departure from the familiar school patterns. This fact will come up again, but its first important implication is for scheduling. Conventional schedules are based chiefly on the requirements of didactic instruction for groups of fixed size. Coaching and seminars, which serve different educational purposes, call for different scheduling and different grouping.

John I. Goodlad, in *A Place Called School* (1983), reported his findings that one-sided didactic talk by teachers dominated most classrooms. He observed students spending more than 80 percent of their class hours in passive listening to teachers and less than 20 percent in active interchanges with them. Even during brief interludes called "discussion" (which Goodlad counted in the 20 percent of the times devoted to active interchanges), teachers were often trying to "cover" a lesson and elicit correct answers to questions of fact. These were quiz sessions, not genuine discussions. What is miscalled "discussion" is simply another form of didactic teaching in which students are only slightly less passive than when silent and listening.

For Paideia teaching, the ratio of passive to active must be altered dramatically and approach an exact reversal of the current situation: 20 percent passive and 80 percent active is the desideratum of the restructured school. It follows from the new empha-

170

sis on learning to use the mind to think, as contrasted with the current emphasis on memorized coverage of subject matter. The students' success in school is to be gauged by a new measure, requiring new uses of the available time, and the traditional weekly grid will not work.

Various schedules are possible, but all will have certain characteristics: they will include options for didactic instruction involving large groups; options for intensive coaching involving small groups; and options for seminars or practicums.

## DEPLOYMENT OF STAFF

School budgets are certain to remain constrained, just as they are now. How, then, can a Paideia school manage to secure a large enough staff to conduct seminars and coaching sessions? For any given personnel budget, new or old, the answer is the same: teachers and other staff members in the school must play multiple roles. They must organize in teams that take advantage of their differing talents.

It is often the case in departmentalized secondary schools that a teacher has the job of instructing 120 or more students in a single subject. From the perspective of the Paideia Program, two undesirable consequences result. *First,* teaching and learning become impersonal. Even though the teacher sees all 120 faces daily, the number is far too great for acquiring a sense of each student's progress, while the student may well spend the time without profit. *Second,* good coaching requires groupings that are much smaller than the typical class size—ideally, one or two students with a tutor; at most six or eight with a coach. For schools to initiate a Paideia Program, two kinds of redeployment are possible. Each must try to solve the twin problems of depersonalization and disconnection through unwieldy groups.

171

At the secondary level, where teachers belong to specialized academic departments, the ratio of students per teacher can be cut in half by the device of pairing two teachers of two related subjects and having each teacher responsible for teaching *both* subjects to one-half the usual number of different students. If a literature teacher were paired with a history teacher, both would teach two subjects—literature *and* history—to 60 students daily rather than one subject to 120 students. This device would permit each teacher to know 60 students well enough to avoid the evils just cited.

Pairing teachers of different subjects would also foster collegiality and teamwork, for coaching and conducting seminars and for training the staff. The paired teachers will help each other prepare instruction in language and history. The one who is better at didactic instruction may take greater responsibility for Column One teaching, allowing the other to devote more time to coaching. Some specialization will still be necessary, but the term should refer to modes of teaching and not to academic subjects. Teams should be organized to conduct all three kinds of teaching, not merely the didactic mode of instruction.

Depending on students' progress, coaching may at times have to occur one-to-one; normally in groups no larger than six or eight. Seminars work best with one or two regularly assigned discussion leaders for a group of 20 to 25. The school will assign as coaches or seminar leaders every competent person in the school community, including administrators and other school staff currently assigned to non-teaching tasks, such as able student-coaches, volunteer parents, and other adults. Everyone associated with the school is a candidate, although most will need additional training to understand and do well in the three kinds of teaching that are explained in Part I of this book.

172

A coaching session in writing might involve a language teacher, a history teacher, an assistant principal, four peer tutors, and a counselor—a team of eight coaches to work with 30–35 students for one or two hours, with the students divided into smaller subgroups according to the skills they need to practice.

If seminar groups run to more than 25, enough students should be assigned the role of observer-critics to lower the number of active participants to 20–25. The critics should listen carefully in order to write an analysis of some aspect of the seminar. This arrangement would be especially useful for students and teachers who are beginners at seminar work and who need criticism to improve their skills.

The two preceding sections on *Schedule* and *Deployment of Staff* discussed ways of restructuring a school's time and reorganizing its personnel in order to make certain that *students* become the center of attention—as active learners, not as passive receivers of delivered instructional services. We now turn to the matter of curriculum.

## CURRICULUM

The Paideia Program aims at a degree of mastery in all subjects and skills that is proportionate to the capacity of each individual student. A Paideia school will be therefore *less* ambitious about comprehensive coverage and *more* ambitious about every student's active engagement in learning.

Let there be no underestimation of this shift of emphasis. It contradicts a trend of many decades. In an essay written as Appendix III to *Paideia Problems and Possibilities*, Theodore Sizer gave helpful advice on how to approach the problem: "Focus on outcomes: what knowledge, skills, and understandings must be demonstrated, at which levels, and how can students most effectively exhibit their mastery? Here again the framework of *The Paideia Proposal* is a starting point, no more than that . . ."

Sizer goes on to say that a good way to do this is to establish tentative checkpoints over the sequence of years planned for the schools, and to work out ways of measuring or assessing accomplishment at each checkpoint. One might select, say, the third, sixth, ninth, and twelfth grade levels (knowing full well that students will reach these different levels at different paces, and thus at moderately differing ages).

This process should bring to the surface disagreements about ends and fuzzy thinking about means. The framework of the three columns is crucial here, for it identifies the products of learning—knowledge, skill, and understanding—to be measured and assessed. How to arrive at such measurement is not easy. What is perfectly clear is that the existing methods are inadequate and, to some degree, meaningless. On this matter, the reader is referred to what is said in the Introduction and in Chapter 16.

In restructuring according to Paideia principles, three guidelines may help to keep the effort on track:

(1) Since students are called upon to use their minds, all other purposes must be subordinated and not allowed to become obstacles to, or distractions from, this main purpose.

(2) Progress and completion should depend more on clear indicators of performance in the three kinds of learning, than on amounts of time spent, credits earned, or age reached.

(3) The principal and teachers should have collective authority to plan the courses of study, choose teaching methods and materials, and schedule time. The more definite, uniform, and integrated the curriculum is, the easier it will be to

handle a flexible schedule and share the responsibility for didactic instruction, coaching, and seminars.

## TRAINING THE STAFF

The Paideia Program will require intensive continuous training of the staff, especially in the period of transition. This training should take place in the school, should be linked closely to the particular tasks that each staff member will be expected to discharge and should, as far as possible, be conducted as part of the regular work week.

The most pressing needs are likely to be these: (1) Immediate and extensive education in any new subject to be taught; (2) training in coaching and in leading seminars, especially for staff members not in regular teaching posts; (3) upgrading of the skills for didactic teaching, though some teachers may not recognize the need; (4) thorough explanations addressed to students, parents, and the public of the philosophy and advantages of a Paideia Program.

One of the reasons for phasing in the Paideia Program over a number of years is to make sure that adequate planning and training smooth the way for each change. Here is Theodore Sizer's counsel on the importance of planning:

> Once under way, time and the means to track the progress of a Paideia school must be built in. Teachers will be threatened, inspired, exhausted, energized, and overwhelmed with the new ways of working. They will need time and opportunity to talk through what their experience is, to re-think approaches which seem not to be working as intended, and to make adjustments in the program. To assume that time for

175

planning and planning again ceases when school starts is a mistake that will harm the program.

Principals and teachers may want to consider these additional suggestions.

(1) Time is precious. Reserve faculty and staff meetings for planning and training actually needed. Use memoranda for routine dissemination of information. Use any mandatory overtime for planning and training, not for usual purposes such as extra-curricular activities.

(2) Use coaching as the main pedagogy for training staff.

(3) Use administrators to replace teachers who are coaching other staff members during the school day.

(4) Curtail the use of temporary substitute teachers. Use the money saved to hire additional permanent teachers, who may then substitute for others and release time for Paideia training; use regular staff to fill in for absent teachers with short illnesses. Make sure that these changes and all personnel policies are incentives for being present in school, not for being absent.

(5) Have teachers and other staff members act as students in coaching and seminar sessions during Paideia training. When possible make video tapes of practice sessions for later critique.

(6) The principal and lead teachers should be willing to do all that they ask their colleagues to do and to show them how they themselves do it.

D.G. & N.C.*

* We are indebted to our colleagues for their contributions to the writing of this chapter: Alonzo Crim, Elizabeth Feely, Richard LaPointe, Ruth Love, and Theodore Sizer. Our special thanks to Julie Love of the Council for Basic Education.

# 15
## How to Recognize a Paideia School

LAST YEAR I met with all the school superintendents in the area of Cincinnati, Ohio, for a question and answer session about *The Paideia Proposal* and *Paideia Problems and Possibilities*. Among the questions asked was one summarized in the title of this chapter: how would an observer know whether a particular school was a Paideia school, putting into practice the Paideia Program?

My answer at that time involved a number of points, some negative, some positive. The negative ones were easy to state. A Paideia school would offer no electives except the choice of a second language. It would not offer any particularized job training of the kind now called "vocational education."

On the positive side, I enumerated the following criteria for judging whether the school had adopted and incorporated the Paideia Program. It would include all twelve years of basic schooling. It would include at all grade levels the three kinds of teaching and of learning as set forth in the three columns of the curricular framework. It would include the three auxiliary subjects: physical education, manual training, and an introduction to the world of work.

In addition, the three kinds of teaching and learning would be found to reverse the present proportions. Now, about 80% to 85% of classroom time from K through 12 is occupied by didactic instruction, the teachers talking uninterruptedly, the students silent and listening passively. Less than 20% of classroom time is devoted to active interchanges between teachers and students, either in coaching sessions or in seminars and discussions. A Paideia school requires a sharp reversal. Active interchanges between teachers and students would occupy 60% to 70% of classroom time, and unrelieved didactic teaching would be kept to 30% to 40%.

But, the most important criterion, first and last, is that a Paideia school provides all its students with equal educational opportunity, equal in quality as in quantity, having one track for all, the same objectives for all, by means of a course of study that is the same for all.

At the same time, those in charge of the curriculum are aware of individual differences in native endowments and in home backgrounds. They administer the same course of study, but in such a way that those who need more help receive supplementary instruction and that everyone achieves as much as his or her individual capacities warrant. This last point involves proportional rather than absolute equality of achievement. For example, unequally endowed students may not accomplish the same amount of learning in such subjects as mathematics or science, but each achieves as much as native capacity allows. All learn some calculus and some physics, but not all learn equal amounts of either.

Having said all this, I reminded my listeners that a Paideia school is recognized by the role played by its principal as its principal teacher and as the educational leader of the school's teaching staff. He is not a mere administrator or paper-pusher.

To conclude, I mentioned a few other facts. A Paideia school has a weekly class schedule that differs from that to be found in most present-day schools. The very classrooms also differ in their configuration for the sake of coaching and seminar work, and so does the use of its teaching staff.

178

When I finished responding to the question in this way, I confessed that this was the best answer that I could give at the time, but that a better answer would be forthcoming. I had in mind this book. Here in the preceding chapters can be found the detailed description of a Paideia school in full operation—what is to be taught, how it is to be taught, and the various restructurings it entails or permits.

One last point: The most striking sign of the presence of a Paideia school is the absence of the present methods of educational score-keeping—of testing, examining, and grading students. So important is this point that it deserves a chapter to itself. It will be found simply by turning the page.

M.J.A.

# 16

## A Note on Grading and the Paradox of Present Practice

THE GRADES we give students on the basis of tests or examinations they take is our way of keeping score in education. The scores we record largely determine whether students pass or fail and whether they graduate from this or that phase of their schooling. For those who do graduate, it determines their rank or standing in the class and the honors they deserve to receive.

The greatest part of this score-keeping measures the amount of information or knowledge acquired. A much smaller part of it measures a second product of learning—the degree of skill developed, mainly in the use of the English language and in performing mathematical operations. Little or none at all measures a third kind of learning—the extent to which a student's understanding has been increased, understanding of the information and knowledge acquired and of basic ideas and issues.

The first kind of learning (acquisition of information and knowledge), aided by didactic teaching with teachers talking, occupies more than 75 percent of classroom time in elementary and secondary schools, and in our colleges as well. The second kind of learning (development of skills) is aided by coaching, which has dwindled to a bare minimum in most of our schools and colleges. The third kind (increase of understanding) is aided by Socratic questioning. This is almost totally absent from most of our schools and colleges; when present, its presence is peripheral and slight.

180

These things being so, it would appear both natural and reasonable for educational score-keeping to place the greatest emphasis on the first kind of learning, the kind that predominates; much less emphasis on the second kind of learning, the kind that has dwindled to the minimum in our schools; and little or none at all to the third kind of learning that is totally absent, or marginal when present.

The paradox in the situation lies in the fact that the first kind of learning is the least durable of all three. The information and knowledge acquired in order to pass tests and examinations is highly transient and evanescent. I have asked the innumerable adult audiences that I have addressed in the last few years about educational matters, how many of those present could now pass the examinations that enabled them years ago to graduate from one or another educational institution and to earn the diplomas, certificates, or degrees they then received. Without exception their response has been that they could not do so now. In fact, most students begin to forget the contents of their courses as soon as the final examination of the year or semester has been taken. Should we not be sorely perplexed by this fact? What is the lasting educational significance of the scores made on tests and examinations of information and knowledge acquired, if most of that information and knowledge is not retained very long after the tests and examinations have been taken?

Skills developed, being habits, not verbal memories, are much more durable than verbally memorized information or knowledge. Yet in our score-keeping we place much less emphasis on our measurement of these accomplishments. It is well known that habits are durable only on condition that they are continually exercised. Not exercised at all, they atrophy. Exercised infrequently, they weaken. That is why language skills are the most durable in all students. Mathematical skills are durable only for

181

those whose professions or occupations require them to use these skills regularly.

We come finally to increased understanding. Of all three kinds of learning, this is the most durable. More than that, it is also *unconditionally* durable. Unlike verbal memories, something understood does not need to be exercised in order to be retained. This, then, is the kind of learning that lasts for a lifetime and is of the greatest importance in the use of our minds and the conduct of our lives. Yet in our educational score-keeping we hardly measure it at all.

Why not? Because this kind of learning is the most difficult to measure. It cannot be accurately assessed by standardized tests or by essay questions to be answered in blue books. The only way it can be sensitively appraised is by an extensive oral examination. This is time consuming and requires great skill in probing the mind of the student—a skill as special as the surgeon's skill in probing the body. The other two kinds of score-keeping, especially the first that dominates the process, are much easier to employ. The easiest way of doing it, of course, is by standardized machine-scoreable tests, but this is also the poorest and least reliable measure of educational accomplishment.

It would be easy to get clear-cut empirical verification of this. Give a class of students in May a series of examinations to test the amount of information and knowledge they have acquired during the academic year just ending, or even the last semester of it. Then, when they return to school in Autumn, give them without any advance warning the same series of examinations. Their scores would show plainly how little they retained over a three-month period. How much less they would retain ten years later!

What do such educational scores measure? Certainly, not the possession of anything of permanent value. What, then? Suppose

182

we grant that they register the willingness, effort, and ability of students to bone up for examinations in order to pass them and get high scores. What of it? Well, since their getting through the years ahead will depend on such willingness, effort, and ability, the scores have some prognostic value for success in their academic and career futures, but for almost nothing else.

If such success consists in acquiring more information and knowledge that they will not long retain, what is the meaning of it for the longer stretch of life itself? In later years, they certainly should be able to look up information they have forgotten and use books to obtain knowledge that cannot be recalled. But what they really need and what would serve them most is their ability to use their minds to size up situations, overcome difficulties, solve problems and to employ their understanding of ideas to direct their lives and deal with life's tangled realities.

The best that can be said for educational score-keeping that relies heavily on tests of information and knowledge acquired is that it may indirectly measure a student's ability to learn. But that must be supplemented by other measures, by wise estimates, which can be arrived at only when the teacher's mind is in direct contact with the student's and when the work they perform together is sustained and involves the two-way communication inherent in coaching and discussion. The Paideia Program calls for this kind of teacher and these modes of teaching. It should therefore yield, from the beginning of school, a far more comprehensive and in the end a more accurate type of score-keeping than is now in use.

M.J.A.

# Recommended Readings
# for Seminars and Other Discussions

THE READINGS here recommended provide materials for (a) seminar discussions, (b) literature classes and language coaching sessions, and (c) supplementary use in subject-matter classes in which textbooks are also used.

They are divided into three sets, as follows. In Set I the readings are intended for children from five to nine years of age, in grades from kindergarten through grade 4. In Set II they are intended for young people from ten to 14 years of age, in grades from 5 through 9. In Set III they are intended for students from 15 to 18 years of age, in grades 10 through 12.

In all three sets, there are easier and more difficult readings. Differences in reading ability may lead teachers to shift certain readings from one set to another, moving more difficult readings to an earlier set or easier readings to a later set. Some of the materials intended for the very young in Set I should be read to the children and then discussed in informal conversations between teachers and pupils.

In all three sets, the recommendations cite the author's name first; then the title of the work (in some cases the title of *part* of that work; in other cases the word "selections" is added in parentheses to indicate that only portions of the work cited are recommended, the selections to be made by the teacher). In all three sets, the order of the recommendations is, first, alphabetical by reference to the initial of the author's last name, and second, divided within the three age groups according to whether the books contain (1) poetry, (2) fables or traditional tales, (3) fiction, (4) plays, (5) books dealing with real people, places, and things, (6) expositions of theory and knowledge, or (7) collections of various kinds.

Each set of recommendations is ample enough to allow teachers to make their own choices. Such choices will have to be made, because more readings are recommended than can possibly be assigned for a given age group or for a given grade between K and 12.

Works of imaginative literature, whether in verse or prose, should be assigned whole rather than partially. Narratives should be read entirely, not one part at a time. With expository literature (science, history, philosophy, etc.), the assignment should seldom, if ever, be the whole work.

A relatively short section of the work suffices and ensures more accurate reading. Sometimes the section to be assigned is indicated; elsewhere the word "selections" leaves the choice of a section up to the teacher.

About the relatively difficult works in Sets II and III, either expository or imaginative, teachers should remember that a first reading is seldom adequate for full comprehension. It should be regarded as a first step toward understanding that which will be attained only through one or more subsequent readings, either in advanced schooling or in adult life. But, no matter how inadequate that first reading of a difficult work may be, it is a mind-opener and a starting point for the growth of understanding.

The discussion of works chosen from these recommended readings should, wherever convenient, provide occasions for coaching students in the skills of reading and others as well—such as the ability to ask and answer questions in discussion. They may also be occasions for asking students to write short essays about the things they have read and discussed, on condition, of course, that the essays submitted are criticized, discussed, and possibly rewritten to improve substance or style or both.

With few exceptions, all works listed can be found on Library of Congress cards, which give complete information. As will become immediately apparent to those readers familiar with the titles listed, many can be found within volumes other than those we have cited. This is not to imply that our selection is preferred; for the sake of brevity, we chose to list only one edition, as opposed to the many that are available.

Those works marked with a * are also available in the Junior Great Books Series, published by Great Books Foundation; ** indicates that we were able to locate the work *only* in the Junior Great Books.

Entries marked with a # are available in the *Gateway to the Great Books* series; ## indicates that we were able to locate the work *only* in the *Gateway* Series.

A very few titles are marked by !!!. This means that our recommendation of the work is not merely suggestive but prescriptive. We regard these readings as mandatory for all future adults who, as citizens of this country, should have some understanding of the basic sources, framework, and principles of our political institutions.

# SET I

## AGES 5 TO 9 YEARS—GRADES K THROUGH 4

### ALPHABETICALLY BY AUTHOR

Verna Aardema, *Who's In Rabbit's House?*
Joy Adamson, *Born Free*
\* Aesop, *Aesop's Fables*
Joan Aiken, *The Kingdom Under the Sea and Other Stories*
Lloyd Alexander, *The Book of Three*
Tony Allan, *The Time Traveller Book of Pharaohs and Pyramids*
Heather Amery, *The Time Traveller Book of Rome and Romans*
Hans Christian Andersen, *Andersen's Fairy Tales*
Mitsumasa Anno, *Anno's Journey*
May H. Arbuthnot (compiled by), *The Arbuthnot Anthology of Children's Literature*
Peter C. Asbjornsen, *East of the Sun and West of the Moon*
Richard & Florence Atwater, *Mr. Popper's Penguins*
\* Ellen C. Babbitt, "The Elephant Girly-Face" and "The Monkey and the Crocodile" from *Jataka Tales: Animal Stories Retold by Ellen C. Babbitt*
Natalie Babbitt, *The Devil's Storybook; Tuck Everlasting*
Betty Baker, *Little Runner of the Longhouse*
Leonard Baskin, *Hosie's Aviary*
Margery Bernstein and Janet Kobrin, *Coyote Goes Hunting for Fire: A California Indian Myth; The First Morning: An African Myth; The Summermaker: An Ojibway Indian Myth*
Stanley and Janice Berenstain, *The Big Honey Hunt*
William Blake, *Songs of Innocence* (selections)
Crosby Newell Bonsall, *Who's A Pest?*
Lindley C. Boyer, *Who Are You?*
Ray Bradbury, "All Summer in a Day"\* and "The Pedestrian" from *Twice Twenty-Two*
Leslie L. Brooke, *Johnny Crow's Garden*

188

*Heywood Broun, *The Fifty-First Dragon*
*Marcia Brown, *Stone Soup*
Margaret Wise Brown, *The Little Fireman; Goodnight Moon*
Jean de Brunhoff, *The Story of Babar*
Bernarda Bryson, *Gilgamesh*
Pearl S. Buck, *The Big Wave*
Ben Lucian Burman, *High Water at Catfish Bend*
Virginia Lee Burton, *The Little House; Mike Mulligan & His Steam Shovel*
Betsy Byars, *The Midnight Fox*
Bennett Cerf, *Bennett Cerf's Book of Riddles*
Richard Chase, *The Jack Tales*
Kornei Chukovskii, *Doctor Powderpill*
Anne Civardi, *The Time Traveller Book of Viking Raiders*
Carlo Collodi, *The Adventures of Pinocchio*
Padraic Colum, *Children of Odin; The Golden Fleece and the Heroes Who Lived Before Achilles*
*Harold Courlander, "Janot Cooks for the Emperor" from *The Piece of Fire and Other Haitian Tales*
Helen Cresswell, *Ordinary Jack*
Albert Cullum, *Aesop in the Afternoon; Shake Hands with Shakespeare; Greek Tears and Roman Laughter*
e.e. cummings, *Fairy Tales*
Edward S. Curtis, *The Girl Who Married a Ghost and Other Tales from the North American Indian*
Roald Dahl, *Charlie and the Chocolate Factory; James and the Giant Peach; The Magic Finger*
Ingri & Edgar P. D'Aulaire, *D'Aulaires' Book of Greek Myths; Norse Gods and Giants*
Meindert DeJong, *The Wheel on the School*
*Walter De La Mare, "Little Red Riding Hood" and "The Turnip" from *Tales Told Again*
*Charlotte Dixon, "Ali Baba and the Forty Thieves" from *Tales from the Arabian Nights*
Glenn J. Doman, *Nose Is Not Toes*

*Appendix*

William Pene Du Bois, *The Twenty-One Balloons*

Gerald Durrell, *My Family and Other Animals*

P. D. Eastman, *A Fish Out of Water; Sam and the Firefly; Are You My Mother?*

Eleanor Estes, *The Hundred Dresses*

Bernard Evslin, *Signs and Wonders: Tales from the Old Testament; Greeks Bearing Gifts: The Epics of Achilles and Ulysses*

Walter Farley, *The Black Stallion; Little Black, a Pony*

*Louise Fatio, *The Happy Lion*

Wanda Gag, *Tales from Grimm; More Tales from Grimm; Millions of Cats; The Funny Thing*

*Rumer Godden, *The Mousewife*

Hardie Gramatky, *Little Toot*

Jacob & Wilhelm Grimm, *Grimm's Fairy Tales*

Elizabeth Guilfoile, *Nobody Listens to Andrew*

J.B.S. Haldane, *My Friend Mr. Leakey*

*Nathaniel Hawthorne, "A Wonder Book" from *A Wonder Book and Tanglewood Tales*

Judy Hindley, *The Time Traveller Book of Knights and Castles*

Syd Hoff, *Danny and the Dinosaur*

Marion Holland, *A Big Ball of String*

Holling C. Holling, *Paddle to the Sea; Tree in the Trail; Seabird; Pagoo*

*Langston Hughes, "Thank You, Ma'm" from *The Langston Hughes Reader*

Dahlov Ipcar, *One Horse Farm*

*Shirley Jackson, "Charles" from *The Lottery*

*Joseph Jacobs, "Jack and the Bean-Stalk" and "Johnny-Cake" from *English Fairy Tales;* "Tattercoats" from *More English Fairy Tales*

Randall Jarrell, *The Animal Family*

William Jaspersohn, *How the Forest Grew*

Norton Juster, *The Phantom Tollbooth*

Mervyn D. Kaufman, *Thomas Alva Edison*

Merriman B. Kaune, *My Own Little House*

Ezra Jack Keats, *Hi, Cat!; The Snowy Day*
Leonard Kessler, *Mr. Pine's Mixed-Up Signs*
Charles Kingsley, *The Heroes*
\*Rudyard Kipling, *Just So Stories*
Phyllis Krasilovsky, *The Very Little Girl*
Ruth Krauss, *I'll Be You - You Be Me; A Hole Is to Dig*
Dorothy Kunhardt, *Pat the Bunny*
\*Albert Lamorisse, *The Red Balloon*
Andrew Lang, *The Blue Fairy Book*
Nancy Larrick, *Piping Down the Valleys Wild*
Robert Lawson, *Rabbit Hill*
Munro Leaf, *The Story of Ferdinand*
Edward Lear, *The Complete Nonsense Book* (selections)
Dennis Lee, *Alligator Pie*
Joan M. Lexau, *Olaf Reads*
Astrid Lindgren, *The Tomten; Pippi Longstocking*
Leo Lionni, *Frederick*
Arnold Lobel, *Mouse Tales; Frog and Toad Are Friends*
\*Hugh Lofting, *The Story of Doctor Doolittle*
Robert Lopshire, *Put Me in the Zoo*
Robert McCloskey, *Make Way for Ducklings; Homer Price*
David McCord, *One at a Time*
George MacDonald, *At the Back of the North Wind*
Spike Milligan, *Silly Verse for Kids*
\*A.A. Milne, *Winnie-the-Pooh*
Else Homelund Minarik, *Little Bear; A Kiss for Little Bear*
Clement C. Moore, *The Night Before Christmas*
Robert Newman, *The Case of the Baker Street Irregular*
Iona and Peter Opie (eds.), *The Oxford Book of Children's Verse; Oxford Nursery Rhyme Book*
Philippa Pearce, *Tom's Midnight Garden*
\*Charles Perrault, *Puss in Boots; Cinderella*
Watty Piper, *The Little Engine That Could*

Beatrix Potter, *The Tale of Peter Rabbit; The Tailor of Gloucester; The Tale of Benjamin Bunny; The Tale of Kim Kitten; The Tale of Mrs. Tiggy-Winkle*

Orville Prescott (ed.), *A Father Reads to His Children*

Alf Prysen, *Little Old Mrs. Pepperpot and Other Stories*

Arthur Ransome, *Old Peter's Russian Tales*

Wilson Rawls, *Where the Red Fern Grows; Summer of the Monkeys*

James Reeves (ed.), *The Merry-Go-Round*

H.A. Rey, *Curious George*

Elizabeth Madox Roberts, *Under the Tree*

Barbara Robinson, *The Best Christmas Pageant Ever*

Marilyn Sachs, *Veronica Ganz*

Felix Salten, *Bambi*

Jose Marie Sanchez-Silva, *The Boy and the Whale*

Carl Sandburg, *The Sandburg Treasury: Prose and Poetry for Young People*

Geoffrey Scott, *Egyptian Boats*

Elizabeth Seeger, *The Ramayana*

George Selden, *The Cricket in Times Square*

Millicent E. Selsam, *When an Animal Grows; Hidden Animals; Let's Get Turtles*

Maurice Sendak, *In the Night Kitchen; Outside Over There*

Dr. Seuss, *Green Eggs and Ham; Cat in the Hat; Hop on Pop; And to Think That I Saw It on Mulberry Street; If I Ran the Zoo*

Shel Silverstein, *Who Wants a Cheap Rhinoceros?; Giraffe and a Half; Where the Sidewalk Ends*

Mary Q. Steele, *Journey Outside*

William Steig, *Dominic; The Real Thief; CDB!; Abel's Island*

Robert Louis Stevenson, *A Child's Garden of Verses*

Frank R. Stockton, *The Best Short Stories of Frank R. Stockton*

Adrien Stoutenburg, *American Tall Tales*

Mildred Taylor, *Roll of Thunder, Hear My Cry*

James Thurber, *Many Moons*

Leo Tolstoy, *Fables and Fairy Tales*

Jim Trelease, *The Read-Aloud Handbook*

* Yoshiko Uchida, "The Terrible Leak" from *Magic Listening Cap; More Folk Tales from Japan;* "The Wedding of the Mouse" from *The Sea of Gold and Other Tales from Japan*

Dorothy Van Woerkem, *Hidden Messages*

Iris Vinton, *Look Out for Pirates*

Clyde Watson, *Father Fox's Pennyrhymes*

Alice Walker, *Langston Hughes, American Poet*

Margery Williams, *The Velveteen Rabbit*

Elizabeth Yates, *Amos Fortune, Free Man*

## POETRY

William Blake, *Songs of Innocence* (selections)

Bennett Cerf, *Bennett Cerf's Book of Riddles*

Langston Hughes, "Thank You, Ma'm" from *The Langston Hughes Reader*

Nancy Larrick, *Piping Down the Valleys Wild*

Dennis Lee, *Alligator Pie*

Spike Milligan, *Silly Verse for Kids*

Clement C. Moore, *The Night Before Christmas*

Iona and Peter Opie (eds.), *The Oxford Book of Children's Verse; Oxford Nursery Rhyme Book*

Carl Sandburg, *The Sandburg Treasury: Prose and Poetry for Young People*

Shel Silverstein, *Who Wants a Cheap Rhinoceros?; Where the Sidewalk Ends*

Robert Louis Stevenson, *A Child's Garden of Verses*

Clyde Watson, *Father Fox's Pennyrhymes*

## MYTHS, FABLES, AND TRADITIONAL TALES

Aesop, *Aesop's Fables*

Hans Christian Andersen, *Andersen's Fairy Tales*

*Appendix*

Ellen C. Babbitt, "The Elephant Girly-Face" and "The Monkey and the Crocodile" from *Jataka Tales: Animal Stories Retold by Ellen C. Babbitt*

Margery Bernstein and Janet Kobrin, *Coyote Goes Hunting for Fire: A California Indian Myth; The First Morning: An African Myth; The Summermaker: An Ojibway Indian Myth*

Marcia Brown, *Stone Soup*

Bernarda Bryson, *Gilgamesh*

Carlo Collodi, *The Adventures of Pinocchio*

Padraic Colum, *Children of Odin; The Golden Fleece and the Heroes Who Lived Before Achilles*

Harold Courlander, "Janot Cooks for the Emperor" from *The Piece of Fire and Other Haitian Tales*

Ingri & Edgar P. D'Aulaire, *D'Aulaires' Book of Greek Myths; Norse Gods and Giants*

Walter De La Mare, "Little Red Riding Hood" and "The Turnip" from *Tales Told Again*

Charlotte Dixon, "Ali Baba and the Forty Thieves" from *Tales from the Arabian Nights*

Bernard Evslin, *Signs and Wonders: Tales from the Old Testament; Greeks Bearing Gifts: The Epics of Achilles and Ulysses*

Wanda Gag, *Tales from Grimm; More Tales from Grimm; Millions of Cats; The Funny Thing*

Jacob & Wilhelm Grimm, *Grimm's Fairy Tales*

Nathaniel Hawthorne, "A Wonder Book" from *A Wonder Book and Tanglewood Tales*

Joseph Jacobs, "Jack and the Bean-Stalk" and "Johnny-Cake" from *English Fairy Tales;* "Tattercoats" from *More English Fairy Tales*

Randall Jarrell, *The Animal Family*

Andrew Lang, *The Blue Fairy Book*

Charles Perrault, *Puss in Boots; Cinderella*

Beatrix Potter, *The Tale of Peter Rabbit; The Tailor of Gloucester; The Tale of Benjamin Bunny; The Tale of Kim Kitten; The Tale of Mrs. Tiggy-Winkle*

Arthur Ransome, *Old Peter's Russian Tales*
Elizabeth Seeger, *The Ramayana*
Shel Silverstein, *Giraffe and a Half*
Adrien Stoutenburg, *American Tall Tales*
Leo Tolstoy, *Fables and Fairy Tales*
Yoshiko Uchida, "The Terrible Leak" from *Magic Listening Cap; More Folk Tales from Japan;* "The Wedding of the Mouse" from *The Sea of Gold and Other Tales from Japan*

## FICTION

Verna Aardema, *Who's in Rabbit's House?*
Joan Aiken, *The Kingdom Under the Sea and Other Stories*
Lloyd Alexander, *The Book of Three*
Mitsumasa Anno, *Anno's Journey*
Peter C. Asbjornsen, *East of the Sun and West of the Moon*
Richard & Florence Atwater, *Mr. Popper's Penguins*
Natalie Babbitt, *The Devil's Storybook; Tuck Everlasting*
Betty Baker, *Little Runner of the Longhouse*
Stanley and Janice Berenstain, *The Big Honey Hunt*
Crosby Newell Bonsall, *Who's a Pest?*
Ray Bradbury, "All Summer in a Day" and "The Pedestrian" from *Twice Twenty-Two*
Leslie L. Brooke, *Johnny Crow's Garden*
Heywood Broun, *The Fifty-First Dragon*
Margaret Wise Brown, *The Little Fireman; Goodnight Moon*
Jean de Brunhoff, *The Story of Babar*
Pearl S. Buck, *The Big Wave*
Ben Lucian Burman, *High Water at Catfish Bend*
Virginia Lee Burton, *The Little House; Mike Mulligan & His Steam Shovel*
Betsy Byars, *The Midnight Fox*
Richard Chase, *The Jack Tales*
Kornei Chukovskii, *Doctor Powderpill*
Helen Cresswell, *Ordinary Jack*

Appendix

Albert Cullum, *Aesop in the Afternoon; Shake Hands with Shakespeare; Greek Tears and Roman Laughter*

e.e. cummings, *Fairy Tales*

Edward S. Curtis, *The Girl Who Married a Ghost and Other Tales from the North American Indian*

Roald Dahl, *Charlie and the Chocolate Factory; James and the Giant Peach; The Magic Finger*

Meindert DeJong, *The Wheel on the School*

William Pene Du Bois, *The Twenty-One Balloons*

Gerald Durrell, *My Family and Other Animals*

P. D. Eastman, *A Fish Out of Water; Sam and the Firefly; Are You My Mother?*

Eleanor Estes, *The Hundred Dresses*

Walter Farley, *The Black Stallion; Little Black, a Pony*

Louise Fatio, *The Happy Lion*

Rumer Godden, *The Mousewife*

Hardie Gramatky, *Little Toot*

Elizabeth Guilfoile, *Nobody Listens to Andrew*

Judy Hindley, *The Time Traveller Book of Knights and Castles*

Syd Hoff, *Danny and the Dinosaur*

Dahlov Ipcar, *One Horse Farm*

Shirley Jackson, "Charles" from *The Lottery*

Norton Juster, *The Phantom Tollbooth*

Merriman B. Kaune, *My Own Little House*

Ezra Jack Keats, *Hi, Cat!; The Snowy Day*

Leonard Kessler, *Mr. Pine's Mixed-Up Signs*

Charles Kingsley, *The Heroes*

Rudyard Kipling, *Just So Stories*

Phyllis Krasilovsky, *The Very Little Girl*

Ruth Krauss, *I'll Be You - You Be Me; A Hole Is to Dig*

Dorothy Kunhardt, *Pat the Bunny*

Albert Lamorisse, *The Red Balloon*

Robert Lawson, *Rabbit Hill*

Munro Leaf, *The Story of Ferdinand*
Edward Lear, *The Complete Nonsense Book* (selections)
Astrid Lindgren, *The Tomten; Pippi Longstocking*
Leo Lionni, *Frederick*
Arnold Lobel, *Mouse Tales; Frog and Toad Are Friends*
*Hugh Lofting, *The Story of Doctor Doolittle*
Robert Lopshire, *Put Me in the Zoo*
Robert McCloskey, *Make Way for Ducklings; Homer Price*
David McCord, *One at a Time*
George MacDonald, *At the Back of the North Wind*
A.A. Milne, *Winnie-the-Pooh*
Else Homelund Minarik, *Little Bear; A Kiss for Little Bear*
Robert Newman, *The Case of the Baker Street Irregular*
Philippa Pearce, *Tom's Midnight Garden*
Watty Piper, *The Little Engine That Could*
Alf Prysen, *Little Old Mrs. Pepperpot and Other Stories*
Wilson Rawls, *Where the Red Fern Grows; Summer of the Monkeys*
H.A. Rey, *Curious George*
Elizabeth Madox Roberts, *Under the Tree*
Barbara Robinson, *The Best Christmas Pageant Ever*
Marilyn Sachs, *Veronica Ganz*
Felix Salten, *Bambi*
Jose Marie Sanchez-Silva, *The Boy and the Whale*
Geoffrey Scott, *Egyptian Boats*
George Selden, *The Cricket in Times Square*
Maurice Sendak, *In the Night Kitchen; Outside Over There*
Dr. Seuss, *Green Eggs and Ham; Cat in the Hat; Hop on Pop; And to
    Think That I Saw it on Mulberry Street; If I Ran the Zoo*
Mary Q. Steele, *Journey Outside*
William Steig, *Dominic; The Real Thief; CDB!; Abel's Island*
Frank R. Stockton, *The Best Short Stories of Frank R. Stockton*
Mildred Taylor, *Roll of Thunder, Hear My Cry*
James Thurber, *Many Moons*

*Appendix*

Dorothy Van Woerkem, *Hidden Messages*
Iris Vinton, *Look Out for Pirates*
Margery Williams, *The Velveteen Rabbit*


BOOKS, CHIEFLY DESCRIPTIVE, ABOUT REAL PEOPLE, PLACES AND
THINGS

Joy Adamson, *Born Free*
Tony Allan, *The Time Traveller Book of Pharaohs and Pyramids*
Heather Amery, *The Time Traveller Book of Rome and Romans*
Leonard Baskin, *Hosie's Aviary*
Anne Civardi, *The Time Traveller Book of Viking Raiders*
J.B.S. Haldane, *My Friend Mr. Leakey*
Holling C. Holling, *Paddle to the Sea; Tree in the Trail; Seabird; Pagoo*
William Jaspersohn, *How the Forest Grew*
Mervyn D. Kaufman, *Thomas Alva Edison*
Millicent E. Selsam, *When an Animal Grows; Hidden Animals; Let's Get
    Turtles*
Alice Walker, *Langston Hughes, American Poet*
Elizabeth Yates, *Amos Fortune, Free Man*


COLLECTIONS

May H. Arbuthnot (compiled by), *The Arbuthnot Anthology of Chil-
    dren's Literature*
Orville Prescott (ed.), *A Father Reads to His Children*
James Reeves (ed.), *The Merry-Go-Round*
Jim Trelease, *The Read-Aloud Handbook*

SET II

AGES 10 TO 14—GRADES 5 THROUGH 9

Frances Hodgson Burnett, *The Secret Garden; Little Lord Fauntleroy*

Shiela Burnford, *The Incredible Journey*

Marilyn Burns, *The Book of Think: Or How to Solve a Problem Twice Your Size*

Lewis Carroll, *Alice's Adventures in Wonderland\*; Through the Looking Glass*

Sidney B. Carroll, *You Be the Judge*

Alice Elizabeth Chase, *Looking at Art*

Apsley George Benet Cherry-Garrard, *The Worst Journey in the World, Antarctic, 1910–1913*

Michael Chinery, *The Living World*

Ann Nolan Clark, *Secret of the Andes; All This Wild Land*

#Joseph Conrad, "Youth" from *Youth and The End of the Tether*

Gale Cooper, *Inside Animals*

James Fenimore Cooper, *The Pioneers; The Last of the Mohicans*

Robert Cormier, *The Chocolate War*

Stephen Crane, *The Red Badge of Courage; The Open Boat, and Three Other Stories\*#*

Richard Cummings, *Make Your Own Model Forts and Castles*

Richard Currier, *Ancient Scrolls*

Richard H. Dana, *Two Years Before the Mast*

Milton Dank, *The Dangerous Game*

#Daniel Defoe, *Robinson Crusoe*

Marie De France, *Shadow of the Hawk and Other Stories*

Meindert De Jong, *Journey from Peppermint Street*

Walter De La Mare, *Come Hither*

Norman Denny & Josephine Filmer-Sankey, *The Bayeux Tapestry: The Story of the Norman Conquest: 1066*

\*Charles Dickens, *A Christmas Carol*

Emily Dickinson, *Poems of Emily Dickinson* (selections)

Arnold Dobrin, *I Am a Stranger on the Earth*

\*Fyodor Dostoevsky, *An Honest Thief, and Other Stories*

Roy Doty, *King Midas Has a Gilt Complex*

William O. Douglas, *Muir of the Mountains*

Arthur Conan Doyle, *The Adventures of Sherlock Holmes*

Donald Elliott and Clinton Arrowood, *Alligators and Music*

Leonard Everett Fisher, *Alphabet Art: Thirteen ABC's from Around the World*

#F. Scott Fitzgerald, "The Diamond as Big as the Ritz" from *Six Tales of the Jazz Age and Other Stories*

Louise Fitzhugh, *Harriet the Spy*

James F. Fixx, *Solve It*

Esther Forbes, *Paul Revere and the World He Lived In; Johnny Tremain*

C.S. Forester, *Captain Horatio Hornblower*

Anne Frank, *Anne Frank: The Diary of a Young Girl*

Jean Fritz, *Homesick: My Own Story; Stonewall*

Robert Frost, *A Swinger of Birches: Poems of Robert Frost for Young People*

Paul Gallico, *The Snow Goose*

Leon Garfield, *Smith*

Leon Garfield & Edward Blishen, *The God beneath the Sea; The Golden Shadow*

Jean Craighead George, *Julie of the Wolves*

Geronimo, *Geronimo's Story of His Life*

*#Nikolai Gogol, "The Overcoat" from *The Overcoat and Other Tales of Good and Evil*

*Kenneth Grahame, *The Wind in the Willows*

*Graham Greene, "The End of the Party" and "The Destructors" from *Collected Stories*

John Gunther, *Alexander the Great*

H. Rider Haggard, *King Solomon's Mines*

E. E. Hale, *The Man Without a Country*

Edith Hamilton, *The Greek Way; The Roman Way*

Ralph Hancock, *Super Machines*

Christie Harris, *Mouse Woman and the Mischief-Makers; Mouse Woman and the Vanished Princesses*

Bret Harte, *The Luck of Roaring Camp*

Appendix

O. Henry, *The Best Short Stories of O. Henry*

Kenneth Heuer, *Rainbows, Halos, and Other Wonders: Light and Color in the Atmosphere*

Thor Heyerdahl, *Kon Tiki; The Ra Expeditions*

Russell Hoban, *How Tom Beat Captain Najork and His Hired Sportsman; The Mouse and His Child*

Margaret Hodges, *The Other World: Myths of the Celts*

Rhoda Hoff, *America's Immigrants: Adventures in Eyewitness History*

Michael Holt, *Maps, Tracks, and the Bridges of Konigsberg*

Washington Irving, *The Sketch Book*

Elizabeth James & Carol Barkin, *What Do You Mean by "Average"?; Means, Medians and Modes*

Will James, *Smoky, the Cow Horse*

Jamie Jobb, *The Night Sky Book*

Samuel Johnson, *Rasselas*

Helen Keller, *The Story of My Life*

M.E. Kerr, *Dinky Hocker Shoots Smack*

Robin Kerrod, *The Universe*

Bettyann Kevles, *Watching the Wild Apes: The Primate Studies of Goodall, Fossey, and Galdikos*

David Kherdian, *Finding Home; The Road from Home*

Rudyard Kipling, *The Jungle Books*

E.L. Konigsburg, *From the Mixed-Up Files of Mrs. Basil E. Frankweiler*

*Jean de La Fontaine, *Fables*

Jean Langton, *The Fledgling*

Ring Lardner, *The Best Short Stories of Ring Lardner*

*#D. H. Lawrence, "The Rocking-Horse Winner" from *The Collected Short Stories of D. H. Lawrence, Vol. 3*

Ursula K. LeGuin, *The Farthest Shore; A Wizard of Earthsea; The Tombs of Atuan*

C.S. Lewis, *The Chronicles of Narnia*

Richard Lewis (ed.), *I Breathe a New Song: Poems of the Eskimo*

Jack London, *The Sea Wolf*; "To Build a Fire"* and "Call of the Wild" from *The Best Stories of Jack London*

Herny Wadsworth Longfellow, *The Poetical Works* (selections)

David Macauley, *Cathedral; City; Castle; Pyramid*

Carson McCullers, *Member of the Wedding*

James Marshall, *Walkabout*

Edgar Lee Masters, *Spoon River Anthology* (selections)

#Guy De Maupassant, "Two Friends" from *Mademoiselle Fifi and Other Stories*

*Prosper Merimee, "Mateo Falcone" in *Great Short Stories of the Modern World*, Barrett H. Clark & Maxim Lieber, eds.

Jean Merrill, *The Pushcart War*

Carolyn Meyer, *Eskimos: Growing Up in a Changing Culture*

Ferdinand N. Monjo, *Letters to Horseface: Being the Story of Wolfgang Amadeus Mozart's Journey to Italy, 1769–1770, When He Was a Boy of Fourteen*

Peter Nabokov (ed.), *Native American Testimony: An Anthology of Indian and White Relations. First Encounter to Dispossession*

Ogden Nash, *Parents Keep Out: Elderly Poems for Youngerly Readers;* "Seeing Eye to Eye Is Believing"* from *Verses from 1929 On*

Gerasenus Nichomachus, *Introduction to Arithmetic*

James Norman, *Ancestral Voices: Decoding Ancient Languages*

Mary Norton, *The Borrowers*

Robert Nye, *Beowulf*

*Frank O'Connor, "My Oedipus Complex" from *Collected Stories*

Scott O'Dell, *Sarah Bishop*

Liam O'Flaherty, "Two Lovely Beasts"* from *Short Stories*

John Parker, *Discovery: Developing Views of the Earth from Ancient Times to Voyages of Captain Cook*

Katherine Paterson, *The Sign of the Chrysanthemum; Of Nightingales That Weep; The Master Puppeteer*

Ann Petry, *Tituba of Salem Village*

Edgar Allan Poe, *Tales of Mystery and Imagination; The Poems of Edgar Allan Poe* (selection)

Howard Pyle, *The Merry Adventures of Robin Hood; Men of Iron*

*Appendix*

Ernest R. Ranucci & Wilma E. Rollins, *Curiosities of the Cube*

Marjorie K. Rawlings, *The Yearling*

Al G. Renner, *How to Make and Use a Microlab*

**Louis B. Saloman, "Univac to Univac"

John G. Samson, *The Pond*

Carl Sandburg, *Early Moon; The Complete Poems of Carl Sandburg* (selections)

*William Saroyan, "The Summer of the Beautiful White Horse" from *My Name Is Aram;* "Gaston" from *Prize Stories 1963: The O. Henry Awards,* Richard Poirier (ed.)

William Shakespeare, *Romeo and Juliet; A Midsummer Night's Dream; Twelfth Night; Othello*

Angela Sheehan, *The Prehistoric World*

Robert Sherwood, *Abe Lincoln in Illinois*

Isaac B. Singer, *A Day of Pleasure: Stories of a Boy Growing Up in Warsaw*

Elizabeth G. Speare, *The Bronze Bow; The Sign of the Beaver; The Witch of Blackbird Pond*

John Steinbeck, "Flight"* from *The Long Valley*

Robert Louis Stevenson, *Treasure Island; The Strange Case of Dr. Jekyll and Mr. Hyde and Other Famous Tales*#

Harriet Beecher Stowe, *Uncle Tom's Cabin*

Mitch Struble, *The Web of Space-Time: A Step-by-Step Exploration of Relativity*

Rosemary Sutcliff, *The Sword and the Circle; The Light Beyond the Forest; Song for a Dark Queen; Blood Feud; The Lantern Bearers; The Witch's Brat; The Shield Ring; Eagle of the Ninth*

James Thurber, *Fables for Our Time*; The Great Quillow*

J.R.R. Tolkien, *The Hobbit*

*Leo Tolstoy, "Master and Man" from *Master and Man and Other Stories*

Pamela L. Travers, *Mary Poppins*

Henry Treece, *The Dream Time*

204

Mark Twain, *The Adventures of Tom Sawyer; The Prince and the Pauper, and Other Stories*

Jules Verne, *Twenty-Thousand Leagues Under the Sea*

#Voltaire, "Micromegas" from *The Portable Voltaire*

*Kurt Vonnegut, Jr., "Harrison Bergeron" from *Welcome to the Monkey House*

H.G. Wells, *The Best Science Fiction Stories; The Time Machine**

Robert Westall, *The Machine Gunners*

E.B. White, *Stuart Little; Charlotte's Web; The Trumpet of the Swan*

John Greenleaf Whittier, *The Poetical Works of Whittier*

*#Oscar Wilde, *The Happy Prince*

Laura Ingalls Wilder, *Little House in the Big Woods; Little House on the Prairie*

Thornton Wilder, *Our Town*

Jay Williams, *Leonardo Da Vinci; Joan of Arc*

Henry Williamson, *Tarka the Otter*

Rose Wyler and Gerald Ames, *It's All Done with Numbers: Astounding and Confounding Feats of Mathematical Magic*

## POETRY

Walter De La Mare, *Come Hither*

Emily Dickinson, *Poems of Emily Dickinson* (selections)

Robert Frost, *A Swinger of Birches: Poems of Robert Frost for Young People*

Richard Lewis (ed.), *I Breathe a New Song: Poems of the Eskimo*

Henry Wadsworth Longfellow, *The Poetical Works* (selections)

Edgar Lee Masters, *Spoon River Anthology* (selections)

Ogden Nash, *Parents Keep Out: Elderly Poems for Youngerly Readers;* "Seeing Eye to Eye Is Believing" from *Verses from 1929 On*

Edgar Allan Poe, *The Poems of Edgar Allan Poe*

Carl Sandburg, *Early Moon; The Complete Poems of Carl Sandburg* (selections)

John Greenleaf Whittier, *The Poetical Works of Whittier*

*Appendix*

## MYTHS, FABLES AND TRADITIONAL TALES

Lucius Apuleius, *The Golden Ass* (selections)

James M. Barrie, *Peter Pan*

John Bierhorst (ed.), *The Red Swan: Myths and Tales of the American Indians; Black Rainbow: Legends of the Incas and Myths of Ancient Peru*

Robert Browning, *The Pied Piper of Hamelin*

Thomas Bulfinch, *Age of Fable*

Paul Gallico, *The Snow Goose*

Leon Garfield, *Smith*

Leon Garfield & Edward Blishen, *The God beneath the Sea; The Golden Shadow*

Margaret Hodges, *The Other World: Myths of the Celts*

Jean de La Fontaine, *Fables*

Robert Nye, *Beowulf*

Katherine Paterson, *The Sign of the Chrysanthemum; Of Nightingales That Weep; The Master Puppeteer*

Howard Pyle, *The Merry Adventures of Robin Hood; Men of Iron*

Rosemary Sutcliff, *The Sword and the Circle; The Light Beyond the Forest; Song for a Dark Queen; Blood Feud; The Lantern Bearers; The Witch's Brat; The Shield Ring; Eagle of the Ninth*

James Thurber, *Fables for Our Time**

## FICTION

Richard Adams, *Watership Down*

Louisa May Alcott, *Little Women*

Hans Christian Andersen, "The Shadow" from *It's Perfectly True and Other Stories*

Isaac Asimov, "The Feeling of Power" from *Nine Tomorrows*

Betty Baker, *Killer-of-Death; Walk on the World's Rim*

L. Frank Baum, *The Wonderful World of Oz; The Wonderful Wizard of Oz*

Ray Bradbury, *The Stories of Ray Bradbury* (esp. "The Veldt")

206

*Recommended Readings*

Pearl S. Buck, *The Good Earth*

Frances Hodgson Burnett, *The Secret Garden; Little Lord Fauntleroy*

Sheila Burnford, *The Incredible Journey*

Lewis Carroll, *Alice's Adventures in Wonderland; Through the Looking Glass*

Ann Nolan Clark, *Secret of the Andes; All This Wild Land*

Joseph Conrad, "Youth" from *Youth and The End of the Tether*

James Fenimore Cooper, *The Pioneers; The Last of the Mohicans*

Robert Cormier, *The Chocolate War*

Stephen Crane, *The Red Badge of Courage; The Open Boat, and Three Other Stories*

Richard H. Dana, *Two Years Before the Mast*

Milton Dank, *The Dangerous Game*

Daniel Defoe, *Robinson Crusoe*

Marie De France, *Shadow of the Hawk and Other Stories*

Meindert De Jong, *Journey from Peppermint Street*

Charles Dickens, *A Christmas Carol*

Fyodor Dostoevsky, *An Honest Thief, and Other Stories*

Roy Doty, *King Midas Has a Gilt Complex*

Arthur Conan Doyle, *The Adventures of Sherlock Holmes*

F. Scott Fitzgerald, "The Diamond as Big as the Ritz" from *Six Tales of the Jazz Age and Other Stories*

Louise Fitzhugh, *Harriet the Spy*

C.S. Forester, *Captain Horatio Hornblower*

Jean Craighead George, *Julie of the Wolves*

Nikolai Gogol, "The Overcoat" from *The Overcoat and Other Tales of Good and Evil*

Kenneth Grahame, *The Wind in the Willows*

Graham Greene, "The End of the Party" and "The Destructors" from *Collected Stories*

H. Rider Haggard, *King Solomon's Mines*

E. E. Hale, *The Man Without a Country*

*Appendix*

Christie Harris, *Mouse Woman and the Mischief-Makers; Mouse Woman and the Vanished Princesses*

Bret Harte, *The Luck of Roaring Camp*

O. Henry, *The Best Short Stories of O. Henry*

Russell Hoban, *How Tom Beat Captain Najork and His Hired Sportsman; The Mouse and His Child*

Washington Irving, *The Sketch Book*

Will James, *Smoky, the Cow Horse*

Samuel Johnson, *Rasselas*

M.E. Kerr, *Dinky Hocker Shoots Smack*

Rudyard Kipling, *The Jungle Books*

E.L. Konigsburg, *From the Mixed-Up Files of Mrs. Basil E. Frankweiler*

Jane Langton, *The Fledgling*

Ring Lardner, *The Best Short Stories of Ring Lardner*

Ursula K. Le Guin, *The Farthest Shore; A Wizard of Earthsea; The Tombs of Atuan*

C.S. Lewis, *The Chronicles of Narnia*

Jack London, *The Sea Wolf;* "To Build a Fire" and "Call of the Wild" from *The Best Stories of Jack London*

Carson McCullers, *Member of the Wedding*

James Marshall, *Walkabout*

Guy De Maupassant, "Two Friends" from *Mademoiselle Fifi and Other Stories*

Prosper Merimee, "Mateo Falcone" in *Great Short Stories of the Modern World*, Barrett H. Clark & Maxim Lieber, eds.

Jean Merrill, *The Pushcart War*

Mary Norton, *The Borrowers*

Frank O'Connor, "My Oedipus Complex" from *Collected Stories*

Liam O'Flaherty, "Two Lovely Beasts" from *Short Stories*

Edgar Allan Poe, *Tales of Mystery and Imagination*

Marjorie K. Rawlings, *The Yearling*

William Saroyan, "The Summer of the Beautiful White Horse" from *My Name Is Aram;* "Gaston" from *Prize Stories 1963: The O. Henry Awards*, Richard Poirier (ed.)

Isaac B. Singer, *A Day of Pleasure: Stories of a Boy Growing Up in Warsaw*

Elizabeth G. Speare, *The Bronze Bow; The Sign of the Beaver; The Witch of Blackbird Pond*

John Steinbeck, "Flight" from *The Long Valley*

Robert Louis Stevenson, *Treasure Island; The Strange Case of Dr. Jekyll and Mr. Hyde and Other Famous Tales*

Harriet Beecher Stowe, *Uncle Tom's Cabin*

James Thurber, *The Great Quillow*

J.R.R. Tolkien, *The Hobbit*

Leo Tolstoy, "Master and Man" from *Master and Man and Other Stories*

Pamela L. Travers, *Mary Poppins*

Henry Treece, *The Dream Time*

Mark Twain, *The Adventures of Tom Sawyer; The Prince and the Pauper, and Other Stories*

Jules Verne, *Twenty-Thousand Leagues Under the Sea*

Voltaire, "Micromegas" from *The Portable Voltaire*

Kurt Vonnegut, Jr., "Harrison Bergeron" from *Welcome to the Monkey House*

H.G. Wells, *The Best Science Fiction Stories; The Time Machine*

Robert Westall, *The Machine Gunners*

E.B. White, *Stuart Little; Charlotte's Web; The Trumpet of the Swan*

Oscar Wilde, *The Happy Prince*

Laura Ingalls Wilder, *Little House in the Big Woods; Little House on the Prairie*

## PLAYS

William Shakespeare, *Romeo and Juliet; A Midsummer Night's Dream; Twelfth Night; Othello*

Robert Sherwood, *Abe Lincoln in Illinois*

Thornton Wilder, *Our Town*

BOOKS, CHIEFLY DESCRIPTIVE, ABOUT REAL PEOPLE,
PLACES AND THINGS

Abigail Adams, *Letters* (selections)
Richard Barber, *A Strong Land and a Sturdy: Life in Medieval England*
P.T. Barnum, *Barnum's Own Story*
Don R. Brothwell, *The Rise of Man*
Walter D. Brownlee, *The First Ships Round the World*
Alice Elizabeth Chase, *Looking at Art*
Apsley George Benet Cherry-Garrard, *The Worst Journey in the World,*
     *Antarctic, 1910–1913*
Michael Chinery, *The Living World*
Gale Cooper, *Inside Animals*
Richard Cummings, *Make Your Own Model Forts and Castles*
Richard Currier, *Ancient Scrolls*
Norman Denny & Josephine Filmer-Sankey, *The Bayeux Tapestry: The*
     *Story of the Norman Conquest: 1066*
William O. Douglas, *Muir of the Mountains*
Leonard Everett Fisher, *Alphabet Art: Thirteen ABC's from Around the*
     *World*
James F. Fixx, *Solve It*
Esther Forbes, *Paul Revere and the World He Lived In; Johnny Tremain*
Anne Frank, *Anne Frank: The Diary of a Young Girl*
Jean Fritz, *Homesick: My Own Story; Stonewall*
Geronimo, *Geronimo's Story of His Life*
John Gunther, *Alexander the Great*
Thor Heyerdahl, *Kon Tiki; The Ra Expeditions*
Rhoda Hoff, *America's Immigrants: Adventures in Eyewitness History*
Jamie Jobb, *The Night Sky Book*
Helen Keller, *The Story of My Life*
Robin Kerrod, *The Universe*
David Kherdian, *Finding Home; The Road from Home*
Carolyn Meyer, *Eskimos: Growing Up in a Changing Culture*
Ferdinand N. Monjo, *Letters to Horseface: Being the Story of Wolfgang*

## Recommended Readings

*Amadeus Mozart's Journey to Italy, 1769–1770, When He Was a Boy of Fourteen*

Peter Nabokov (ed.), *Native American Testimony: An Anthology of Indian and White Relations. First Encounter to Dispossession*

James Norman, *Ancestral Voices: Decoding Ancient Languages*

John Parker, *Discovery: Developing Views of the Earth from Ancient Times to Voyages of Captain Cook*

Ann Petry, *Tituba of Salem Village*

Ernest R. Ranucci & Wilma E. Rollins, *Curiosities of the Cube*

John G. Samson, *The Pond*

Angela Sheehan, *The Prehistoric World*

Jay Williams, *Leonardo Da Vinci; Joan of Arc*

Henry Williamson, *Tarka the Otter*


### EXPOSITIONS OF THEORY AND KNOWLEDGE

Norman D. Anderson, *Investigating Science in the Swimming Pool and Ocean; Investigating Science Using Your Whole Body*

Louise Armstrong, *How to Turn Up into Down into Up: A Child's Guide to Inflation, Depression and Economic Recovery*

Melvin Berger, *Quasars, Pulsars, and Black Holes in Space; Tools of Modern Biology*

Kees Boeke, *Cosmic View*

Marilyn Burns, *The Book of Think: Or How to Solve a Problem Twice Your Size*

Edith Hamilton, *The Greek Way; The Roman Way*

Ralph Hancock, *Super Machines*

Kenneth Heuer, *Rainbows, Halos, and Other Wonders: Light and Color in the Atmosphere*

Michael Holt, *Maps, Tracks, and the Bridges of Konigsberg*

Elizabeth James & Carol Barkin, *What Do You Mean by "Average"?; Means, Medians and Modes*

Bettyann Kevles, *Watching the Wild Apes: The Primate Studies of Goodall, Fossey, and Galdikos*

*Appendix*

Gerasenus Nichomachus, *Introduction to Arithmetic*
Al G. Renner, *How to Make and Use a Microlab*
Louis B. Saloman, "Univac to Univac"
Mitch Struble, *The Web of Space-Time: A Step-by-Step Exploration of Relativity*
Rose Wyler and Gerald Ames, *It's All Done with Numbers: Astounding and Confounding Feats of Mathematical Magic*

212

# SET III

## AGES 15 TO 18—GRADES 10 THROUGH 12

### ALPHABETICALLY BY AUTHOR

Edwin A. Abbott, *Flatland*

#Henry Adams, *History of the United States of America During the Administrations of Jefferson and Madison* (Vol. 1, Chapters I & VI)

!!!Mortimer Adler and William Gorman, *The American Testament*

Mortimer Adler & Charles Van Doren, *How to Read a Book*

Aeschylus, *Prometheus Bound; The Oresteia; Seven Against Thebes*

Archimedes, "The Sand-Reckoner" and "On Floating Bodies" (Book I) from *Great Books of the Western World*, v.11

Aristophanes, *The Clouds; The Birds; The Frogs; Lysistrata*

Aristotle, *Nicomachean Ethics, Book I; Politics, Book I; Poetics*

#Matthew Arnold, "The Study of Poetry" and "Sweetness and Light" from *Matthew Arnold: Poetry and Prose*

W.H. Auden, *Collected Poems* (selections)

St. Augustine, *The Confessions of Augustine*, Bks. I–VII

Marcus Aurelius, *Meditations*

Jane Austen, *Pride and Prejudice; Emma; Sense and Sensibility*

#Francis Bacon, "Of Beauty," "Of Discourse," "Of Great Places," "Of Marriage and the Single Life," "Of Parents and Children," "Of Seditions and Troubles," "Of Studies," and "Of Youth and Age," from *Essays;* "The Sphinx"##

James A. Baldwin, *The Fire Next Time*

#Honoré de Balzac, "A Passion in the Desert" from *Short Stories*

Samuel Beckett, *Waiting for Godot*

E.T. Bell, *Men of Mathematics*

Saul Bellow, *The Adventures of Augie March*

Claude Bernard, "Experimental Considerations Common to Living Things and Inorganic Bodies," from *An Introduction to the Study of Experimental Medicine* (Ch. III)

William Blake, *Songs of Innocence and Songs of Experience* (selections)

*Appendix*

Percy W. Bridgman, *The Logic of Modern Physics*

Charlotte Brontë, *Jean Eyre*

Emily Brontë, *Wuthering Heights*

#Sir Thomas Browne, *Hydriotaphia (Urn Burial)*, (Ch. V: "Immortality")

Robert Browning, *The Complete Poetical Works of Browning* (selections)

#Ivan Bunin, "The Gentleman from San Francisco" from *The Gentleman from San Francisco and Other Stories*

Robert Burns, *The Poetical Works of Burns* (selections)

#J. B. Bury, "Herodotus" from *The Ancient Greek Historians*

George G. Byron, *The Poetical Works of Byron* (selections)

Huntington Cairns (ed.), *The Limits of Art*

!!! #John C. Calhoun, "The Concurrent Majority" from *A Disquisition on Government*

#Tommasso Campanella, *The Defense of Galileo of Thomas Campanella*

#Norman Robert Campbell, "Measurement" and "Numerical Laws and the Use of Mathematics in Science" from *What Is Science?* (Chapters VI and VII)

#Thomas Carlyle, "The Hero as King" (Lecture VI) from *On Heroes, Hero-Worship, and the Heroic in History*

Rachel Carson, "The Sunless Sea"# from *The Sea Around Us; Silent Spring*

Henry Cavendish, "Experiments with Air" from *The Scientific Papers of the Honourable Henry Cavendish*

Miguel de Cervantes, *Don Quixote*

Geoffrey Chaucer, *Canterbury Tales*

#Anton P. Chekhov, *The Cherry Orchard;* "The Darling" from *The Portable Chekhov;* "The Pulp" and "The Evildoer" from *Shadows and Light*

#M.T. Cicero, *On Old Age and On Friendship*

Arthur C. Clarke, *Childhood's End*

#Carl Von Clausewitz, "What Is War?" from *On War* (Chapter 1)

#William K. Clifford, "The Postulates of the Science of Space" in *The World of Mathematics*, v.1, James R. Newman, ed. "The Ethics of Belief" in *Religion from Tolstoy to Camus*, W.A. Kauffman (ed.)

Samuel Taylor Coleridge, *The Poems of Samuel Taylor Coleridge* (selections)

Joseph Conrad, *Heart of Darkness and the Secret Sharer;* "Youth"# from *Youth and The End of the Tether*

!!! #J. Hector St. John de Crevecoeur, *Letters from an American Farmer and Sketches of Eighteenth-Century America*, Letter III, "The Making of Americans"

#Eve Curie, *Madame Curie*

Dante, "That Mankind Needs Unity and Peace"# from *Monarchy*, Bk. I

#Tobias Dantzig, "Fingerprints" and "The Empty Column" from *Number: The Language of Science* (Chapters I and II)

Charles Darwin, *Autobiography of Charles Darwin#; Voyage of the "Beagle"*

Paul DeKruif, *Microbe Hunters*

#Thomas DeQuincey, "The Literature of Knowledge and the Literature of Power" and "On the Knocking at the Gate in Macbeth" in *The Oxford Anthology of English Literature*, Vol. 2

#John Dewey, *How We Think: A Restatement of the Relation of Reflective Thinking to the Educative Process*

Charles Dickens, *David Copperfield; Great Expectations; Oliver Twist*

Emily Dickinson, *Poems of Emily Dickinson* (selections)

Annie Dillard, *Pilgrim at Tinker Creek*

Isak Dinesen, *Winter's Tales*

John Donne, *Complete Poems* (selections)

Fyodor Dostoevsky, *Crime and Punishment*

#Sir Arthur Eddington, "The Running-down of the Universe" from *The Nature of the Physical World* (Chapter IV)

#Albert Einstein & Leopold Infeld, "The Rise and Decline of Classical Physics" from *The Evolution of Physics*

#Loren Eiseley, "On Time" from *The Immense Journey*

George Eliot, *Middlemarch; Silas Marner; Adam Bede*

\#T.S. Eliot, "Dante" and "Tradition and the Individual Talent" from *Selected Essays; Complete Poems and Plays* (selections)

Ralph Ellison, *The Invisible Man*

\#Ralph Waldo Emerson, "Thoreau," "Nature," "Self-Reliance," and "Montaigne; or, The Skeptic" from *Essays; Poems of Ralph Waldo Emerson* (selections)

Epictetus, *Enchiridion#; Discourses* (2 Vols.)

\#Epicurus, "Letter to Herodotus" and "Letter to Menoeceus" from *Letters, Principal Doctrines and Vatican Sayings*

\#John Erskine, "The Moral Obligation to Be Intelligent" from *The Moral Obligation to Be Intelligent and Other Essays*

Euclid, Book I from *The Elements* (Vol. 1)

\#Leonhard Euler, "The Seven Bridges of Konigsberg" in *The World of Mathematics*, v. 1, James R. Newman (ed.)

Euripides, *Medea; The Bacchae; Hippolytus*

\#Henri Fabre, *The Life of the Fly* (Ch. 1); *The Sacred Beetle and Others* (selections); *The Glow-Worm and Other Beetles*

Clifton Fadiman (ed.), *The Mathematical Magpie; Fantasia Mathematica*

\#Michael Faraday, *The Chemical History of a Candle;* "Observations on Mental Education"\#\#

William Faulkner, *Collected Stories of William Faulkner*

Henry Fielding, *Tom Jones*

F. Scott Fitzgerald, *Six Tales of the Jazz Age and Other Stories; The Great Gatsby*

Gustave Flaubert, *Madame Bovary*

\#\#Andre Russell Forsyth, "Mathematics in Life and Thought"

!!! \#Benjamin Franklin, *The Autobiography of Benjamin Franklin;* "A Proposal for Promoting Useful Knowledge among the British Plantations in America" and "Proposals Relating to the Education of Youth in Pennsylvania" in *Three Thousand Years of Educational Wisdom*, Robert Ulich (ed.)

Robert Frost, *The Poetry of Robert Frost* (selections)

Carlos Fuentes, *Where the Air Is Clear; The Death of Artemio Cruz*

##Galileo Galilei, "The Starry Messenger"

#Francis Galton, *Hereditary Genius* (Introduction, Chapters I, II)

George Gamow, *One, Two, Three . . . Infinity; Biography of the Earth, Its Past, Present and Future; Biography of Physics; Mr. Tompkins Explores the Atom; Birth and Death of the Sun; Mr. Tompkins in Wonderland*

Gabriel Garcia-Marquez, *One Hundred Years of Solitude*

Edward Gibbon, *The Decline and Fall of the Roman Empire* (Chapters 15 & 16)

Johann W. Von Goethe, *Faust: Part I*

William Golding, *Lord of the Flies*

Samuel Gompers, *Seventy Years of Life and Labour* (2 Volumes)

Nadine Gordimer, *Selected Stories*

Stephen Jay Gould, *The Panda's Thumb: More Reflections in Natural History*

Ulysses S. Grant, *Personal Memoirs*

Robert Graves, *I, Claudius*

#Francois Guizot, "Civilization" from *History of Civilization in Europe* (Lecture I)

#J.B.S. Haldane, "On Being the Right Size" in *The World of Mathematics*, v. 2, James R. Newman (ed.)

!!!Alexander Hamilton, et al., *The Federalist Papers*, Nos. I–X

Geoffrey H. Hardy, *A Mathematician's Apology*

Thomas Hardy, *The Complete Poems* (selections)

William Harvey, "Circulation of the Blood" from *Circulation of the Blood and Other Writings*

Nathaniel Hawthorne, *The Scarlet Letter; Twice-Told Tales*

#William Hazlitt, "My First Acquaintance with Poets," "On Swift," "Of Persons One Would Wish to Have Seen," and "On the Feeling of Immortality in Youth" from *Selected Essays*

Robert A. Heinlein, *The Moon Is a Harsh Mistress*

218

Sir James Jeans, "Beginnings and Endings" from *The Universe Around Us* (Chapter VII)

!!! #Thomas Jefferson, "The Declaration of Independence," "First Inaugural Address," and "Notes on Virginia" (Query XIII: 'The Constitution of the State and Its Several Charters') from *The Life and Selected Writings of Thomas Jefferson*

#Samuel Johnson, "Preface to Shakespeare" from *Rasselas, Poems, and Selected Prose*

James Joyce, *A Portrait of the Artist as a Young Man*

Franz Kafka, *The Trial; The Castle; The Complete Stories*

#Immanuel Kant, *Perpetual Peace*

#Edward Kasner & James R. Newman, "New Names for Old" and "Beyond the Googol" from *Mathematics and the Imagination*

John Keats, *The Poems of John Keats* (selections)

!!!Martin Luther King, "I Have a Dream" in *The World's Great Speeches*, Lewis Copeland and Lawrence Lamm (eds.)

Arthur Koestler, *Darkness at Noon*

#Jean de La Bruyère, *Characters*

#Charles Lamb, "My First Play," "Dream Children, a Reverie," and "Sanity of True Genius" from *Essays of Elia* (bound with *Last Essays of Elia*)

#Pierre S. Laplace, *A Philosophical Essay on Probabilities* (Chapters I–IV)

Antoine Lavoisier, *Elements of Chemistry* (Part I) in *Great Books of the Western World*, v. 45

*#D.H. Lawrence, "The Rocking-Horse Winner" from *The Collected Short Stories of D.H. Lawrence*, Vol. 3

C.S. Lewis, *Out of the Silent Planet; That Hideous Strength; Perelandra*

Sinclair Lewis, *Babbitt; Main Street*

#Abraham Lincoln, "Address at Cooper Institute," "First Inaugural Address," "Letter to Horace Greeley," "Meditation on the Divine Will," "Address at the Dedication of the Gettysburg National Cemetery," "Second Inaugural Address," and "Last Public Address" from *The Life and Writings of Abraham Lincoln*

*Appendix*

Charles A. Lindbergh, *The Spirit of St. Louis*

John Locke, *A Letter Concerning Toleration; Second Treatise of Government*, Chapters I–IV

##Lucian, "The Way to Write History"

Lucretius, *On the Nature of Things*, Books I–IV

#Sir Charles Lyell, "Geological Evolution" from *Principles of Geology* (Vol. III: Chapter I)

#Thomas B. Macaulay, "Machiavelli" from *Critical and Historical Essays*

Niccolo Machiavelli, *The Prince*

Archibald MacLeish, *New and Collected Poems* (selections)

#Thomas Robert Malthus, "The Principle of Population" from *Population: The First Essay* (Chapters I–IV)

#Thomas Mann, *Stories of Three Decades*

Karl Marx & Frederick Engels, *The Communist Manifesto*

Herman Melville, *Billy Budd;#  Moby Dick;#* "Bartleby" and "Benito Cereno" from *The Piazza Tales*

#Dmitri Mendeleev, "The Periodic Law of the Chemical Elements" in *The World of Mathematics*, v. 2, James R. Newman (ed.)

#John Stuart Mill, *On Liberty; Considerations on Representative Government* (Chapters I–VI); "Childhood and Youth" from *Autobiography of John Stuart Mill*

Arthur Miller, *The Crucible*

John Milton, *Areopagitica*

Jean B. Molière, "The Misanthrope,"# "Tartuffe," and "The Doctor in Spite of Himself"# from *Misanthrope and Other Plays*

Michel de Montaigne, *Montaigne: Selections from the Essays*

V.S. Naipaul, *Miguel Street; A House for Mr. Biswas; An Area of Darkness*

Pablo Neruda, *Selected Poems of Pablo Neruda* (selections)

James R. Newman (ed.), *The World of Mathematics*

Isaac Newton, *Optics*, Book III and "The System of the World," from *Principia Mathematica*, both in *Great Books of the Western World*, v. 34

\*Frank O'Connor, "My Oedipus Complex" from *Collected Stories*

\*Liam O'Flaherty, "Two Lovely Beasts" from *Short Stories*

Eugene O'Neill, *The Emperor Jones;# The Iceman Cometh;* "Mourning Becomes Electra" from *Three Plays*

George Orwell, *1984; Animal Farm*

!!!Thomas Paine, "Common Sense" and "The American Crisis" (No. I: 'A Call to Patriots') from *Common Sense and Other Political Writings*

#Walter H. Pater, "The Art of Life" from *The Renaissance*

Alan Paton, *Cry, the Beloved Country*

#Ivan P. Pavlov, "Scientific Study of the So-Called Psychical Processes in the Higher Animals," from *Conditioned Reflexes: An Investigation of the Physiological Activity of the Cerebral Cortex* (Chapter 4)

#Charles S. Peirce, "The Red and the Black" in *The World of Mathematics*, v. 2, James R. Newman (ed.)

Plato, *Euthyphro, Apology, and Crito;\* Symposium; Phaedrus; The Republic*, Bks. I & II

Pliny the Younger, Letter LXV 'To Tacitus,'# and Letter LXVI, 'To Cornelius Tacitus,'# from "Letters" in *The Harvard Classics*, v. 9; *Letters of Marcus Tullius Cicero, with His Treatises on Friendship and Old Age; Letters of Gaius Plinius Caecilius Secundus*

Plutarch, *The Lives of the Noble Grecians and Romans;* "Contentment" and "Of Bashfulness" from the *Moralia##*

#Henri Poincaré, 'Space,' from "Science and Hypothesis" (Chapters III–V) and 'Mathematical Creation' (Chapter III) and 'Chance' from "Science and Method" (Chapter IV) in *The Foundations of Science: Science and Hypothesis, the Value of Science, Science and Method*

Alexander Pope, "An Essay on Man" and "An Essay on Criticism" from *The Poems of Alexander Pope*

#William H. Prescott, "The Land of Montezuma" from *The Conquest of Mexico*

*Appendix*

Joseph Priestley, *Experiments and Observations on Different Kinds of Air*, Vol. 2

Ptolemy, *The Almagest* (Book I, Ch. 1–8) in *Great Books of the Western World*, v. 16

#Alexander Pushkin, "The Queen of Spades" from *Prose Tales*

François Rabelais, *Gargantua and Pantagruel* (Books I–IV)

John Crowe Ransom, *Selected Poems* (selections)

E.A. Robinson, *Complete Poems* (selections)

Jean-Jacques Rousseau, *Social Contract* (Book I)

#John Ruskin, "An Idealist's Arraignment of the Age" from *Fors Clavigera, Letters to the Workmen and Labourers of Great Britain* (Letter V)

#Bertrand Russell, "The Study of Mathematics" and "Mathematics and the Metaphysicians" from *Mysticism and Logic and Other Essays* (Chapters IV and V); "Definition of Number"# from *Introduction to Mathematical Philosophy* (Chapter II)

#Charles Sainte-Beuve, "What Is a Classic?" and "Montaigne" from *Literary and Philosophical Essays*

J.D. Salinger, *The Catcher in the Rye; Nine Stories*

George Santayana, *Three Philosophical Poets;#* "The Unknowable" from *Obiter Scripta*

#Friedrich Schiller, "On Simple and Sentimental Poetry" from *Essays Aesthetical and Philosophical*

#Arthur Schopenhauer, "On Style," "On Education," "On Some Forms of Literature," and "On the Comparative Place of Interest and Beauty in Works of Art" from *Complete Essays of Schopenhauer; Seven Books in One Volume*

George I. Schwartz (ed.), *Moments of Discovery*

William Shakespeare, *Hamlet; As You Like It; Julius Caesar; The Sonnets*

#George Bernard Shaw, "Candida" and "The Man of Destiny" from *Plays: Pleasant and Unpleasant*, v. 2; *Major Barbara; Pygmalion; Saint Joan*

#Percy B. Shelley, "A Defence of Poetry," from *The Selected Poetry and Prose of Percy Bysshe Shelley; The Poetical Works of Shelley* (selections)

Richard B. Sheridan, *The School for Scandal;#* The Rivals

Isaac B. Singer, *The Spinoza of Market Street and Other Stories; Gimpel the Fool and Other Stories*

Adam Smith, "Introduction and Plan of the Work" and "Of the Profits of Stock" (Chapter 9, Book I) from *The Wealth of Nations*

*Sophocles, *Antigone; Oedipus the King; Philoctetes*

Olaf Stapeldon, "Last and First Men" from *Last and First Men and Star Maker;* "Odd John" from *Odd John and Sirius*

John Steinbeck, *The Grapes of Wrath; The Red Pony*

#Robert Louis Stevenson, "The Lantern-Bearers" from *Across the Plains, with Other Memories and Essays*

Jonathan Swift, *Gulliver's Travels;* "A Meditation Upon a Broom-Stick,"# "When I Come to Be Old,"# and "A Modest Proposal"# from *Eighteenth-Century English Literature,* Geoffrey Tilotson (comp.); "An Essay on Modern Education"##

#John M. Synge, "Riders to the Sea" from *Complete Plays of John M. Synge*

Leo Szilard, *The Voice of the Dolphins, and Other Stories*

Cornelius Tacitus, *Annals of Imperial Rome;* "The Life of Gnaeus Julius Agricola"# from *The Agricola and the Germania*

Alfred L. Tennyson, *Poetical Works of Tennyson* (selections)

Dylan Thomas, *Collected Poems* (selections)

Lewis Thomas, *The Lives of a Cell: Notes of a Biology Watcher; The Medusa and the Snail; Late Night Thoughts on Listening to Mahler's Ninth Symphony*

Henry David Thoreau, "Walden," "Civil Disobedience,"# and "A Plea for Captain John Brown"# from *Walden and Other Writings of Henry David Thoreau*

Thucydides, *The Peloponnesian War* (Books I & II)

James Thurber, *My World—And Welcome To It*

*Appendix*

Alexis de Tocqueville, *Democracy in America* (In Vol. I: Introduction, Ch. III, IV, XI–XIV, Conclusion; in Vol. II: Book II, Ch. I–IV; Book III, Ch. VII–XII)

Leo Tolstoy, *War and Peace; The Death of Ivan Ilyich;#* *Twenty-Three Tales#*

George M. Trevelyan, "Clio" from *Clio, a Muse and Other Essays*

Barbara W. Tuchman, *The Guns of August*

Ivan Turgenev, *Fathers and Sons;* "First Love"# and "Mumu"* from *First Love and Other Tales*

Mark Twain, *Huckleberry Finn; Short Stories of Mark Twain;#* "Learning the River"# from *Life on the Mississippi* (Ch. 1, 4, 6–14)

John Tyndall, *Faraday as a Discoverer* (Ch. I–III)#

René Vallery-Radot, *The Life of Pasteur*

Carl Van Doren, *Benjamin Franklin*

Mark Van Doren, *Collected and New Poems, 1924–1963* (selections); *Shakespeare*

Virgil, *The Aeneid of Virgil*

Voltaire, *Candide;* Letters VIII–XVII, XXIII and XXIV from *Letters on England; The Portable Voltaire* (selected essays #)

Robert Penn Warren, *All the King's Men; Selected Poems, 1923–1975*

#George Washington, "The Farewell Address" and "On Disbanding the Army" in *The People Shall Judge*, v. 1

T.H. White, *The Once and Future King*

#Alfred North Whitehead, "On Mathematical Method" from *An Introduction to Mathematics* (Chapters I–III); "On the Nature of A Calculus" from *A Treatise on Universal Algebra with Applications* (Chapter I)

Walt Whitman, "The Death of Abraham Lincoln"# from *Walt Whitman; Leaves of Grass* (selections)

William Carlos Williams, *Selected Poems of William Carlos Williams*

##Friedrich Wohler, "On the Artificial Production of Urea"

Virginia Woolf, *A Room of One's Own;* "How Should One Read A Book?"# and "The Art of Biography"# from *Collected Essays*

224

Recommended Readings

William Wordsworth, *The Complete Poetical Works of Wordsworth* (selections)

Richard Wright, *Black Boy: A Record of Childhood and Youth*

#Xenophon, "The March to the Sea" from *Xenophon's Anabasis* (Book IX); "The Character of Socrates" from *Xenophon's Memorabilia of Socrates* (Book IV)

William Butler Yeats, *Collected Poems* (selections)

POETRY

W.H. Auden, *Collected Poems* (selections)

William Blake, *Songs of Innocence and Songs of Experience* (selections)

Robert Browning, *The Complete Poetical Works of Browning* (selections)

Robert Burns, *The Poetical Works of Burns* (selections)

George G. Byron, *The Poetical Works of Byron* (selections)

Geoffrey Chaucer, *Canterbury Tales*

Samuel Taylor Coleridge, *The Poems of Samuel Taylor Coleridge* (selections)

Emily Dickinson, *Poems of Emily Dickinson* (selections)

John Donne, *Complete Poems* (selections)

T.S. Eliot, *Complete Poems and Plays* (selections)

Ralph Waldo Emerson, *Poems of Ralph Waldo Emerson* (selections)

Robert Frost, *The Poetry of Robert Frost* (selections)

Johann W. Von Goethe, *Faust: Part I*

Thomas Hardy, *The Complete Poems* (selections)

Homer, *The Iliad; The Odyssey*

Langston Hughes, *The Big Sea; Selected Poems of Langston Hughes; The Langston Hughes Reader*

John Keats, *The Poems of John Keats* (selections)

Lucretius, *On the Nature of Things*, Books I–IV

Archibald MacLeish, *New and Collected Poems* (selections)

Pablo Neruda, *Selected Poems of Pablo Neruda* (selections)

*Appendix*

Alexander Pope, "An Essay on Man" and "An Essay on Criticism" from *The Poems of Alexander Pope*
John Crowe Ransom, *Selected Poems* (selections)
E.A. Robinson, *Complete Poems* (selections)
William Shakespeare, *The Sonnets*
Percy B. Shelley, *The Poetical Works of Shelley* (selections)
Alfred Lord Tennyson, *Poetical Works of Tennyson* (selections)
Dylan Thomas, *Collected Poems* (selections)
Mark Van Doren, *Collected and New Poems, 1924–1963* (selections); *Shakespeare*
Virgil, *The Aeneid of Virgil*
Robert Penn Warren, *Selected Poems, 1923–1975*
Walt Whitman, "The Death of Abraham Lincoln" from *Walt Whitman; Leaves of Grass* (selections)
William Carlos Williams, *Selected Poems of William Carlos Williams*
William Wordsworth, *The Complete Poetical Works of Wordsworth* (selections)
William Butler Yeats, *Collected Poems* (selections)

## Myths, Fables, and Traditional Tales

Jean de La Bruyère, *Characters*
Lucian, "The Way to Write History"
George Orwell, *Animal Farm*

## Fiction

Jane Austen, *Pride and Prejudice; Emma; Sense and Sensibility*
Honoré de Balzac, "A Passion in the Desert" from *Short Stories*
Saul Bellow, *The Adventures of Augie March*
Charlotte Brontë, *Jane Eyre*
Emily Brontë, *Wuthering Heights*
Ivan Bunin, "The Gentleman from San Francisco" from *The Gentleman from San Francisco and Other Stories*

Recommended Readings

Miguel de Cervantes, *Don Quixote*

Anton P. Chekhov, "The Darling" from *The Portable Chekhov;* "The Pulp" and "The Evildoer" from *Shadows and Light*

Arthur C. Clarke, *Childhood's End*

Joseph Conrad, *Heart of Darkness and the Secret Sharer;* "Youth" from *Youth and The End of the Tether*

Charles Dickens, *David Copperfield; Great Expectations; Oliver Twist*

Annie Dillard, *Pilgrim at Tinker Creek*

Isak Dinesen, *Winter's Tales*

Fyodor Dostoevsky, *Crime and Punishment*

George Eliot, *Middlemarch; Silas Marner; Adam Bede*

Ralph Ellison, *The Invisible Man*

William Faulkner, *Collected Stories of William Faulkner*

Henry Fielding, *Tom Jones*

F. Scott Fitzgerald, *Six Tales of the Jazz Age and Other Stories; The Great Gatsby*

Gustave Flaubert, *Madame Bovary*

Carlos Fuentes, *Where the Air Is Clear; The Death of Artemio Cruz*

Gabriel Garcia-Marquez, *One Hundred Years of Solitude*

William Golding, *Lord of the Flies*

Nadine Gordimer, *Selected Stories*

Robert Graves, *I, Claudius*

Nathaniel Hawthorne, *The Scarlet Letter; Twice-Told Tales*

Robert A. Heinlein, *The Moon Is a Harsh Mistress*

Joseph Heller, *Catch Twenty-Two*

Ernest Hemingway, *The Old Man and the Sea; A Farewell to Arms; For Whom the Bell Tolls; Short Stories of Ernest Hemingway*

Richard Hughes, *A High Wind in Jamaica*

Aldous Huxley, *Brave New World;* "Young Archimedes" from *Collected Short Stories*

Shirley Jackson, *The Lottery*

Henry James, *The American; The Ambassadors; The Portrait of a Lady*

*Appendix*

James Joyce, *A Portrait of the Artist as a Young Man*
Franz Kafka, *The Trial; The Castle; The Complete Stories*
Arthur Koestler, *Darkness at Noon*
D.H. Lawrence, "The Rocking-Horse Winner" from *The Collected Short Stories of D.H. Lawrence,* Vol. 3
C.S. Lewis, *Out of the Silent Planet; That Hideous Strength; Perelandra*
Sinclair Lewis, *Babbitt; Main Street*
Thomas Mann, *Stories of Three Decades*
Herman Melville, *Billy Budd; Moby Dick;* "Bartleby" and "Benito Cereno" from *The Piazza Tales*
V.S. Naipaul, *Miguel Street; A House for Mr. Biswas; An Area of Darkness*
Frank O'Connor, "My Oedipus Complex" from *Collected Stories*
Liam O'Flaherty, "Two Lovely Beasts" from *Short Stories*
George Orwell, *1984*
Alan Paton, *Cry, the Beloved Country*
Alexander Pushkin, "The Queen of Spades" from *Prose Tales*
François Rabelais, *Gargantua and Pantagruel* (Books I–IV)
J.D. Salinger, *The Catcher in the Rye; Nine Stories*
Isaac B. Singer, *The Spinoza of Market Street and Other Stories; Gimpel the Fool and Other Stories*
Olaf Stapeldon, "Last and First Men" from *Last and First Men and Star Maker;* "Odd John" from *Odd John and Sirius*
John Steinbeck, *The Grapes of Wrath; The Red Pony*
Robert Louis Stevenson, "The Lantern-Bearers" from *Across the Plains, with Other Memories and Essays*
Jonathan Swift, *Gulliver's Travels*
Leo Tolstoy, *War and Peace; The Death of Ivan Ilyich; Twenty-Three Tales*
Ivan Turgenev, *Fathers and Sons;* "First Love" and "Mumu" from *First Love and Other Tales*
Mark Twain, *Huckleberry Finn; Short Stories of Mark Twain;* "Learning the River" from *Life on the Mississippi* (Ch. 1, 4, 6–14)
Robert Penn Warren, *All the King's Men*

228

T.H. White, *The Once and Future King*
Richard Wright, *Black Boy: A Record of Childhood and Youth*

## PLAYS

Aeschylus, *Prometheus Bound; The Oresteia; Seven Against Thebes*
Aristophanes, *The Clouds; The Birds; The Frogs; Lysistrata*
Samuel Beckett, *Waiting for Godot*
Anton P. Chekhov, *The Cherry Orchard*
Euripides, *Medea; The Bacchae; Hippolytus*
Du Bose Heyward, *Porgy*
Henrik Ibsen, *An Enemy of the People; Ghosts; A Doll's House; The Wild Duck; Hedda Gabler*
Arthur Miller, *The Crucible*
Jean B. Molière, "The Misanthrope," "Tartuffe," and "The Doctor in Spite of Himself" from *Misanthrope and Other Plays*
Eugene O'Neill, *The Emperor Jones; The Iceman Cometh;* "Mourning Becomes Electra" from *Three Plays*
William Shakespeare, *Hamlet; As You Like It; Julius Caesar*
George Bernard Shaw, "Candida" and "The Man of Destiny" from *Plays: Pleasant and Unpleasant*, v. 2; *Major Barbara; Pygmalion; Saint Joan*
Richard B. Sheridan, *The School for Scandal; The Rivals*
Sophocles, *Antigone; Oedipus the King; Philoctetes*
John M. Synge, "Riders to the Sea" from *Complete Plays of John M. Synge*

## BOOKS, CHIEFLY DESCRIPTIVE, ABOUT REAL PEOPLE, PLACES, AND THINGS

Henry Adams, *History of the United States of America During the Administrations of Jefferson and Madison* (Vol. 1, Chapters I & VI)
St. Augustine, *The Confessions of Augustine*, Bks. I–VII
J. B. Bury, "Herodotus" from *The Ancient Greek Historians*
Rachel Carson, "The Sunless Sea" from *The Sea Around Us; Silent Spring*

*Appendix*

M.T. Cicero, *On Old Age and On Friendship*

J. Hector St. John de Crèvecoeur, *Letters from an American Farmer and Sketches of Eighteenth-Century America*, Letter III, "The Making of Americans"

Eve Curie, *Madame Curie*

Charles Darwin, *Autobiography of Charles Darwin; Voyage of the "Beagle"*

Leonhard Euler, "The Seven Bridges of Konigsberg" in *The World of Mathematics*, v. 1, James R. Newman (ed.)

Henri Fabre, *The Life of the Fly* (Ch. 1); *The Sacred Beetle and Others* (selections); *The Glow-Worm and Other Beetles*

Benjamin Franklin, *The Autobiography of Benjamin Franklin;* "A Proposal for Promoting Useful Knowledge among the British Plantations in America" and "Proposals Relating to the Education of Youth in Pennsylvania" in *Three Thousand Years of Educational Wisdom*, Robert Ulich, ed.

Edward Gibbon, *The Decline and Fall of the Roman Empire* (Chapters 15 & 16)

Samuel Gompers, *Seventy Years of Life and Labour* (2 Volumes)

Ulysses S. Grant, *Personal Memoirs*

Herodotus, *The Histories*, Books I & II

John Hersey, *Hiroshima*

Charles A. Lindbergh, *The Spirit of St. Louis*

Plutarch, *The Lives of the Noble Grecians and Romans;* "Contentment" and "Of Bashfulness" from the *Moralia*

William H. Prescott, "The Land of Montezuma" from *The Conquest of Mexico*

Cornelius Tacitus, *Annals of Imperial Rome;* "The Life of Gnaeus Julius Agricola" from *The Agricola and the Germania*

Thucydides, *The Peloponnesian War* (Books I & II)

James Thurber, *My World—And Welcome To It*

Barbara W. Tuchman, *The Guns of August*

John Tyndall, *Faraday as a Discoverer* (Ch. I–III)

Recommended Readings

René Vallery-Radot, *The Life of Pasteur*
Carl Van Doren, *Benjamin Franklin*
Xenophon, "The March to the Sea" from *Xenophon's Anabasis* (Book IX);
    "The Character of Socrates" from *Xenophon's Memorabilia of
    Socrates* (Book IV)
*Historical Documents:*
    "The English Bill of Rights" (v. 1)
    "The Virginia Declaration of Rights" (v. 1)
    "The Declaration of Independence" (v. 1)
    "The Constitution of the United States" (v. 1)
    "The Charter of the United Nations" (v. 2)
    "Universal Declaration of Human Rights" (v. 2) in *The People Shall
        Judge*
    "Declaration of the Rights of Man and of Citizen"


EXPOSITIONS OF THEORY AND KNOWLEDGE

Edwin A. Abbott, *Flatland*
Mortimer Adler and William Gorman, *The American Testament*
Mortimer Adler & Charles Van Doren, *How to Read a Book*
Archimedes, "The Sand-Reckoner" and "On Floating Bodies" (Book I)
    from *Great Books of the Western World*, v. 11
Aristotle, *Nicomachean Ethics, Book I; Politics, Book I; Poetics*
Matthew Arnold, "The Study of Poetry" and "Sweetness and Light" from
    *Matthew Arnold: Poetry and Prose*
Marcus Aurelius, *Meditations*
Francis Bacon, "Of Beauty," "Of Discourse," "Of Great Places," "Of
    Marriage and the Single Life," "Of Parents and Children," "Of
    Seditions and Troubles," "Of Studies," and "Of Youth and Age,"
    from *Essays;* "The Sphinx"
James A. Baldwin, *The Fire Next Time*
E.T. Bell, *Men of Mathematics*
Claude Bernard, "Experimental Considerations Common to Living Things

231

and Inorganic Bodies," from *An Introduction to the Study of Experimental Medicine* (Ch. III)

Percy W. Bridgman, *The Logic of Modern Physics*

Sir Thomas Browne, Ch. V, "Immortality" from *Hydriotaphia* (Urn Burial)

Huntington Cairns (ed.), *The Limits of Art*

John C. Calhoun, "The Concurrent Majority" from *A Disquisition on Government*

Tommasso Campanella, *The Defense of Galileo of Thomas Campanella*

Norman Robert Campbell, "Measurement" and "Numerical Laws and the Use of Mathematics in Science" from *What Is Science?* (Chapters VI and VII)

Thomas Carlyle, "The Hero as King" (lecture VI) from *On Heroes, Hero-Worship, and the Heroic in History*

Henry Cavendish, "Experiments with Air" from *The Scientific Papers of the Honourable Henry Cavendish*

Carl Von Clausewitz, "What Is War?" from *On War* (Chapter 1)

William K. Clifford, "The Postulates of the Science of Space" in *The World of Mathematics*, v. 1, James R. Newman (ed.); "The Ethics of Belief" in *Religion from Tolstoy to Camus*, W.A. Kauffman (ed.)

Dante, "That Mankind Needs Unity and Peace" from *Monarchy*, Bk. I

Tobias Dantzig, "Fingerprints" and "The Empty Column" from *Number: The Language of Science* (Chapters I and II)

Thomas DeQuincey, "The Literature of Knowledge and the Literature of Power" and "On the Knocking at the Gate in Macbeth" in *The Oxford Anthology of English Literature*, Vol. 2

John Dewey, *How We Think: A Restatement of the Relation of Reflective Thinking to the Educative Process*

Sir Arthur Eddington, "The Running-down of the Universe" from *The Nature of the Physical World* (Chapter IV)

Albert Einstein & Leopold Infeld, "The Rise and Decline of Classical Physics" from *The Evolution of Physics*

Loren Eiseley, "On Time" from *The Immense Journey*

T.S. Eliot, "Dante" and "Tradition and the Individual Talent" from *Selected Essays*

Ralph Waldo Emerson, "Thoreau," "Nature," "Self-Reliance," and "Montaigne; or, The Skeptic" from *Essays*

Epictetus, *Enchiridion; Discourses* (2 Vols.)

Epicurus, "Letter to Herodotus" and "Letter to Menoeceus" from *Letters, Principal Doctrines and Vatican Sayings*

John Erskine, "The Moral Obligation to Be Intelligent" from *The Moral Obligation to Be Intelligent and Other Essays*

Euclid, Book I from *The Elements* (Vol. 1)

Clifton Fadiman (ed.), *The Mathematical Magpie; Fantasia Mathematica*

Michael Faraday, *The Chemical History of a Candle;* "Observations on Mental Education"##

Andrew Russell Forsyth, "Mathematics, in Life and Thought"

Galileo Galilei, "The Starry Messenger"

Francis Galton, *Hereditary Genius* (Introduction, Chapters I, II)

George Gamow, *One, Two, Three . . . Infinity; Biography of the Earth, Its Past, Present and Future; Biography of Physics; Mr. Tompkins Explores the Atom; Birth and Death of the Sun; Mr. Tompkins in Wonderland*

Stephen Jay Gould, *The Panda's Thumb: More Reflections in Natural History*

François Guizot, "Civilization" from *History of Civilization in Europe* (Lecture I)

J.B.S. Haldane, "On Being the Right Size" in *The World of Mathematics,* v. 2, James R. Newman (ed.)

Alexander Hamilton, et al., *The Federalist Papers,* Nos. I–X

Geoffrey H. Hardy, *A Mathematician's Apology*

William Harvey, "Circulation of the Blood" from *Circulation of Blood and Other Writings*

William Hazlitt, "My First Acquaintance with Poets," "On Swift," "Of Persons One Would Wish to Have Seen," and "On the Feeling of

Immortality in Youth" from *Selected Essays*

H.L.F. von Helmholtz, "On the Conservation of Force" from *The Harvard Classics*, v. 30: *Scientific Papers*

Eugene Herrigel, *Zen in the Art of Archery*

Lancelot Hogben, "Mathematics, the Mirror of Civilization," from *Mathematics for the Million*

David Hume, "Of Refinement in the Arts," "Of Money," "Of the Balance of Trade," and "Of Taxes" from *Writings on Economics;* "Of the Standard of Taste" from *The Harvard Classics,* v. 27: *English Essays from Sir Philip Sidney to Macaulay;* "Of the Study of History"

Thomas H. Huxley, "On the Relations of Man to the Lower Animals" from *Man's Place in Nature and Other Essays;* "On a Piece of Chalk" from *Oxford Anthology of English Prose*

William James, "The Will to Believe," "The Sentiment of Rationality," and "Great Men and Their Environment" from *The Will to Believe and Other Essays in Popular Philosophy;* "On a Certain Blindness in Human Beings" and "The Energies of Men" from *Essays on Faith and Morals*

Sir James Jeans, "Beginnings and Endings" from *The Universe Around Us* (Chapter VII)

Thomas Jefferson, "The Declaration of Independence," "First Inaugural Address," and "Notes on Virginia" (Query XIII: 'The Constitution of the State and Its Several Charters') from *The Life and Selected Writings of Thomas Jefferson*

Samuel Johnson, "Preface to Shakespeare" from *Rasselas, Poems, and Selected Prose*

Immanuel Kant, *Perpetual Peace*

Edward Kasner & James R. Newman, "New Names for Old" and "Beyond the Googol" from *Mathematics and the Imagination*

Martin Luther King, "I Have a Dream" in *The World's Great Speeches,* Lewis Copeland and Lawrence Lamm (eds.)

Charles Lamb, "My First Play," "Dream Children, a Reverie," and "San-

234

ity of True Genius" from *Essays of Elia* (bound with *Last Essays of Elia*)

Pierre S. Laplace, *A Philosophical Essay on Probabilities* (Chapters I–IV)

Antoine Lavoisier, *Elements of Chemistry* (Part I) in *Great Books of the Western World,* v. 45

Abraham Lincoln, "Address at Cooper Institute," "First Inaugural Address," "Letter to Horace Greeley," "Meditation on the Divine Will," "Address at the Dedication of the Gettysburg National Cemetery," "Second Inaugural Address," and "Last Public Address" from *The Life and Writings of Abraham Lincoln*

John Locke, *A Letter Concerning Toleration; Second Treatise of Government,* Chapters I–IV

Sir Charles Lyell, "Geological Evolution" from *Principles of Geology* (Vol. III: Chapter I)

Thomas B. Macaulay, "Machiavelli" from *Critical and Historical Essays*

Niccolo Machiavelli, *The Prince*

Thomas Robert Malthus, "The Principle of Population" from *Population: The First Essay* (Chapters I–V)

Karl Marx & Frederick Engels, *The Communist Manifesto*

Dmitri Mendeleev, "The Periodic Law of the Chemical Elements" in *The World of Mathematics,* v. 2, James R. Newman (ed.)

John Stuart Mill, *On Liberty; Considerations on Representative Government* (Chapters I–VI); "Childhood and Youth" from *Autobiography of John Stuart Mill*

John Milton, *Areopagitica*

Michel de Montaigne, *Montaigne: Selections from the Essays*

James R. Newman (ed.), *The World of Mathematics*

Isaac Newton, *Optics,* Book III  and "The System of the World" from *Principia Mathematica,* both in *Great Books of the Western World,* v. 34

Thomas Paine, "Common Sense" and "The American Crisis" (No. I: 'A

Call to Patriots') from *Common Sense and Other Political Writings*

Walter H. Pater, "The Art of Life" from *The Renaissance*

Ivan P. Pavlov, "Scientific Study of the So-Called Psychical Processes in the Higher Animals," from *Conditioned Reflexes: An Investigation of the Physiological Activity of the Cerebral Cortex* (Chapter 4)

Charles S. Peirce, "The Red and the Black" in *The World of Mathematics*, v. 2, James R. Newman (ed.)

Plato, *Euthyphro, Apology, and Crito; Symposium; Phaedrus; The Republic*, Bks. I & II

Pliny the Younger, Letter LXV, 'To Tacitus,' and Letter LXVI, 'To Cornelius Tacitus,' from "Letters" in *The Harvard Classics*, v. 9; *Letters of Marcus Tullius Cicero, with His Treatises on Friendship and Old Age; Letters of Gaius Plinius Caecilius Secundus*

Henri Poincaré, 'Space,' from "Science and Hypothesis" (Chapters III–V) and 'Mathematical Creation' (Chapter III) and 'Chance' from "Science and Method" (Chapter IV) in *The Foundations of Science: Science and Hypothesis, the Value of Science, Science and Method*

Joseph Priestley, *Experiments and Observations on Different Kinds of Air*, Vol. 2

Ptolemy, *The Almagest* (Book I, Ch. 1–8) in *Great Books of the Western World*, v. 16

Jean-Jacques Rousseau, *Social Contract* (Book I)

John Ruskin, "An Idealist's Arraignment of the Age" from *Fors Clavigera, Letters to the Workmen and Labourers of Great Britain* (Letter V)

Bertrand Russell, "The Study of Mathematics" and "Mathematics and the Metaphysicians" from *Mysticism and Logic and Other Essays* (Chapters IV and V); "Definition of Number" from *Introduction to Mathematical Philosophy* (Chapter II)

Charles Sainte-Beuve, "What Is a Classic?" and "Montaigne" from *Literary and Philosophical Essays*

George Santayana, *Three Philosophical Poets;* "The Unknowable" from *Obiter Scripta*

Friedrich Schiller, "On Simple and Sentimental Poetry" from *Essays Aesthetical and Philosophical*

Arthur Schopenhauer, "On Style," "On Education," "On Some Forms of Literature," and "On the Comparative Place of Interest and Beauty in Works of Art" from *Complete Essays of Schopenhauer; Seven Books in One Volume*

Percy B. Shelley, "A Defence of Poetry," from *The Selected Poetry and Prose of Percy Bysshe Shelley*

Adam Smith, "Introduction and Plan of the Work" and "Of the Profits of Stock" (Chapter 9, Book I) from *The Wealth of Nations*

Jonathan Swift, "A Meditation Upon a Broom-Stick," "When I Come to Be Old," and "A Modest Proposal" from *Eighteenth-Century English Literature,* Geoffrey Tilotson (comp.); "An Essay on Modern Education"##

Lewis Thorbas, *The Lives of a Cell: Notes of a Biology Watcher; The Medusa and the Snail; Late Night Thoughts on Listening to Mahler's Ninth Symphony*

Henry David Thoreau, "Walden," "Civil Disobedience," and "A Plea for Captain John Brown" from *Walden and Other Writings of Henry David Thoreau*

Alexis de Tocqueville, *Democracy in America* (In Vol. I: Introduction, Ch. III, IV, XI–XIV, Conclusion; in Vol. II: Book II, Ch. I–IV; Book III, Ch. VII–XII.)

George M. Trevelyan, "Clio" from *Clio, a Muse and Other Essays*

Voltaire, *Candide;* Letters VIII–XVII, XXIII and XXIV from *Letters on England; The Portable Voltaire* (selected essays)

George Washington, "The Farewell Address" and "On Disbanding the Army" in *The People Shall Judge,* v. 1

Alfred North Whitehead, "On Mathematical Method" from *An Introduc-*

*tion to Mathematics* (Chapters I–III); "On the Nature of a Cal-
culus" from *A Treatise on Universal Algebra with Applications*
(Chapter I)
Friedrich Wohler, "On the Artificial Production of Urea"
Virginia Woolf, *A Room of One's Own;* "How Should One Read a Book?"
and "The Art of Biography" from *Collected Essays*

Made in the USA
Middletown, DE
19 March 2021

35780332R00151